HILLSIDE
LANDSCAPING

BY SUSAN LANG AND THE EDITORS OF SUNSET BOOKS

SUNSET BOOKS · MENLO PARK, CALIFORNIA

A POSITIVE SLANT

The idea of landscaping a hillside may be disconcerting at first, especially if you're accustomed to gardening on level ground—but it needn't be. Whether your starting point is a barren or weedy slope or an existing landscape that demands change, be assured that there's something wonderful you can do with your hillside. You have only to thumb through the following pages to see many of the splendid, and often ingenious, possibilities.

This book provides the information you need to tackle your slope with confidence. You'll learn about aesthetic as well as technical aspects of hillside landscaping, so that your slope is beautiful *and* stable. And if you're short of ideas, the pictorial tour offered in the second chapter is sure to spark your imagination.

For their assistance in preparing this book, we gratefully acknowledge the following people: Scott Fitzgerrell for reviewing the chapter on building; Ryan Fortini and Scott Atkinson for their help on water features and decks, respectively; and Victor Thomas of Lyngso Garden Materials, Redwood City, California, for his advice.

SUNSET BOOKS

Vice President, General Manager: Richard A. Smeby
Vice President, Editorial Director: Bob Doyle
Production Director: Lory Day
Director of Operations: Rosann Sutherland
Art Director: Vasken Guiragossian

Staff for this book:

Managing Editor: Susan Bryant Caron
Sunset Books Senior Editor: Marianne Lipanovich
Copy Editor: Julie Harris
Proofreader: Alicia Eckley
Indexer: Nanette Cardon
Production Coordinator: Danielle Javier

Art Director: Alice Rogers
Illustrator: Rik Olson
Computer Production: Susan Bryant Caron

Cover: Photography by Marion Brenner. Photo styling by Cynthia Del Fava. Border photograph by Crandall & Crandall.

PHOTOGRAPHERS:

Marion Brenner: 10 top, 11 top, 25 top left, 35 bottom left, 37 bottom right, 38 top, 41 bottom right, 49 top right, 50 bottom left, 51 bottom right, 55 bottom, 56 top, 63 top right, bottom left, 70 top left, 83 bottom; **Karen Bussolini:** 18 bottom, 29 bottom right, 30 bottom right, 31 bottom left, 32 top left, top right, 35 bottom right, 39 top left, 43 bottom, 48 bottom right, 49 bottom left, 57 top right, 58 top right, 59 top left, bottom left, bottom right, 60 top, 65 middle, bottom, 69 bottom right, 74 top, 80 bottom, 81 top left, 88 middle, 122 top; **David Cavagnaro:** 27 bottom, 50 bottom right, 77 top right, bottom right, 126 top, middle; **Connie Coleman:** 26 top right; **Glenn Cormier:** 32 bottom left; **Alan & Linda Detrick:** 17 middle right, 22 top, 36 top left, 52 middle right, 61 top left, bottom right, 65 top, 81 top right; **William Dewey:** 88 top; **Derek Fell:** 7 bottom right, 9, 27 top, 45 top left, 46 top left, 51 top right, middle right, 58 bottom left, 73 bottom left, 82, 102, 113, 124 middle; **Steven Gunther:** 1, 94 bottom; **Harry Haralambou:** 6 bottom, 33 top right, 52 middle left, 58 top left, 67 top right, bottom right, 107 top; **Pamela Harper:** 107 bottom, 128; **Marcus Harpur:** 83 top; **Philip Harvey:** 8 top, 29 top left, bottom, 30 bottom left, 35 top, 36 bottom left, bottom right, 39 top right; **Saxon Holt:** 2, 3 top left, 4, 17 bottom, 23 middle, 25 top right, 26 top left, 28, 31 bottom left, 34 top, 37 top, 39 bottom left, 45 top right, 47 bottom left, 55 middle right, 61 top right, 63 top left, 64 bottom left, 69 bottom left, 70 middle right, 76 bottom, 81 bottom left, bottom right, 84 middle, 87, 99, 105; **James Frederick Housel:** 24 bottom left, 44 bottom right, 55 top; **Dency Kane:** 7 top, 11 bottom, 57 bottom right, 62 middle right, 63 bottom right, 72 bottom left, 95; **Suzanne Kelso:** 37 bottom left; **Michael Landis:** 3 bottom left, 34 bottom left, 46 bottom left, 52 top right, 53 bottom right, 55 middle left, 66, 67 top left, 74 bottom, 76 top, 86, 120, 125 top, back cover bottom left; **Janet Loughrey:** 117; **Allan Mandell:** 7 middle, 22 bottom, 38 bottom, 40 bottom right, 42 bottom, 48 top left, 52 bottom right, 62 middle left, bottom left, 64 top left, 71 middle left, 73 top left, top right, 94 top, 124 top right; **Charles Mann:** 3 bottom left, 8 bottom, 17 middle left, 19 top, 24 bottom right, 26 bottom left, 39 bottom right, 42 top left, top right, 43 top right, 60 bottom, 71 middle right, 75 bottom left, 77 top left, 90, 112, 118, 123 top, bottom left; **Jim McCausland:** 122 bottom; **David McDonald:** 3 middle left, 7 bottom left, 41 top left, 47 top, 54 top, bottom left, 62 top, 68 bottom left, 78, 104; **Jack McDowell:** 56 bottom, 111; **Chas McGrath:** 21 bottom, 127; **Terrence Moore:** 64 bottom right, 67 bottom left; **Richard Nicol:** 34 bottom right, 36 top right, 44 top; **Jerry Pavia:** 41 top left, 45 bottom left, 50 top, 51 middle left, 53 bottom left, 61 bottom left, 68 top right, 69 top left, top right, 70 bottom left, 71 top, bottom right, 72 top, bottom right, 75 top left, 89, 101, 124 top left, bottom; **PhotoGarden, Inc.:** 25 bottom, 41 bottom left, 46 top right, 53 top right, 70 bottom right; **Norman A. Plate:** 47 bottom right, 53 top left, 54 bottom right, 126 bottom; **Sandra Lee Reha:** 17 top, 19 bottom left, bottom right, 57 bottom left, 58 bottom right, back cover right; **Bill Ross:** 40 top, 49 top left; **Susan A. Roth:** 3 top right, 6 top, 14, 18 top left, top right, 21 top left, 23 bottom, 31 top right, 33 top left, 46 bottom right, 48 bottom left, 49 bottom right, 68 bottom right, 73 bottom right, 75 top right, bottom right, 84 top, bottom, 93, 125 bottom; **Judith Ryan:** 20; **Richard Shiell:** 48 top right, 51 top left, 64 top right; **Robyn Shotwell:** 10 bottom; **Lauren Springer:** 26 bottom right; **Michael S. Thompson:** 16, 21 top right, 23 top, 24 top left, top right, 29 top right, 31 top left, 32 bottom right, 33 top left, 43 top left, 52 top left, 57 top left, 77 bottom left, 80 top back cover top left; **Walpole Woodworkers, Inc.:** 59 top right; **Western Red Cedar Lumber Association:** 30 top, 108; **Peter O. Whiteley:** 44 bottom left, 45 bottom right; **Tom Woodward:** 123 bottom right.

CONTENTS

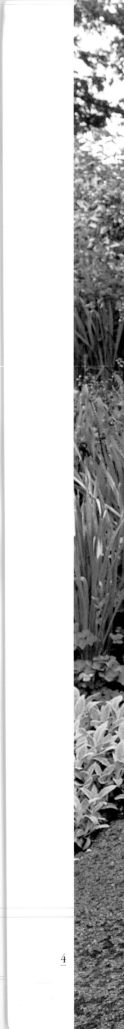

Slopes generally make for more interesting landscapes than flat terrain. In fact, garden designers often create changes in elevation on level lots to add a visually appealing "third dimension" to the properties.

UNDERSTANDING YOUR
TERRAIN

Even though hillsides may pose challenges to anyone planting or building on them, they also offer many landscaping opportunities. For example, a gully created by runoff is a choice spot for a dry creekbed; a blustery bluff cries out for a windbreak; and a strip of level land near the house is ideal for a patio. Study your terrain for clues to how best to proceed. Also consider how your intended modifications will affect the hillside. On a slight slope, the impact of landscaping may also be slight. But a steep or unstable slope may have to be shored up with retaining walls to prevent the newly installed landscape from washing away in the first heavy rainstorm.

You may be able to create the landscape you want without reshaping the land. But if you do recontour, remember— the more drastic the changes, the costlier the landscaping will be and the more attention must be devoted to drainage and erosion control.

Colorful perennials and bulbs blanket a moderate front slope.

TYPES OF HILLSIDES

The term "hillside" applies to shallow slopes as well as precipitous ones. Some lots slope gently enough that very few allowances must be made for the grade—even lawn may be grown on the slant without posing a mowing problem. The grade doesn't have to steepen much, however, before turf becomes impractical, giving way to alternatives such as ground covers. As the pitch increases, retaining walls and stairways are commonly incorporated to make the land usable for gardening or outdoor living.

Even very steep hillsides can be made productive. Just look at lushly landscaped homes clinging to San Francisco peaks, where terracing has transformed narrow, steep yards into multilevel, secluded retreats in the middle of a crowded city. Or, go farther afield, to the Incan mountainside city of Machu Picchu in Peru or the traditional hillside villas and gardens in countries bordering the Mediterranean Sea. In these places, too, terracing has tamed sharp slopes. Many of the stone terraces there are still intact after centuries of holding back hillsides.

Your hillside property may not be as dramatic as those described above, but it probably has some interesting features that can contribute to a satisfying landscape. Examine your lot to see how it slopes and how it sits in relation to neighboring properties. (Hillside lots differ radically, even in a subdivision where they were all graded at the same time, so what worked for your neighbor may not work for you.) Keep an eye peeled for

Creating terraced stone retaining walls—like these at the Alhambra in Granada, Spain—is a traditional way to make very steep slopes practical for gardening.

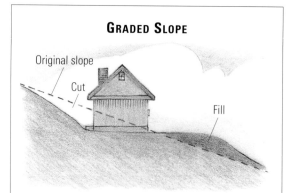

GRADED SLOPE

Original slope

Cut

Fill

Many hilly lots are graded when the land is developed for housing. The slope is cut to create a new grade, and the excavated soil is used to fill another part of the original slope. The purpose is to create a level area for the house and usually a patio and lawn. Ideally, the house is constructed on cut soil rather than compacted fill.

On a very gentle slope, lawn and beds are easy to plant and maintain.

Dense plantings cover this moderate incline accented with fieldstones and low rock walls.

Outcroppings on this moderately steep, rocky slope have been incorporated into the landscape.

landscaping opportunities, as well as for any features that you may have to mitigate.

Perhaps your property is a suburban lot that was graded when the house was built and has mostly level ground, a gentle bank down to the street, and an abrupt upward slope at the rear of the lot. With such a property, you have flattish land for a patio and easily accessible planting beds, yet there are slopes for vertical relief.

On the other hand, your property may be situated on a natural or minimally graded slope that slants upward or downward from the street. You may wish to preserve the character of the slope with a natural-looking landscape featuring plants that are native or well adapted to your area. A steep downward slope behind the house is ideal for a private deck cantilevered over the hill, while a sharp upward slope right behind the house may compel you to locate a deck more publicly, streetside.

Many sites slope in two directions. For example, on a street that runs up a slope, each lot sits higher than the one below and all the lots may have steep backyards that slope sharply upward or downward toward lots on adjacent streets. In such a case, your landscaping plans may include structures or plants that create privacy from uphill neighbors or screen your views downhill.

Or, instead of sloping at a uniform rate, your land may be so irregular that it is best described as undulating or rolling. If you despair at such uneven terrain, consider that landscapers create mounds and depressions on flat land to give it interest—your land has interest built in. You may want to smooth out part of the slope to make planting or building on it easier, but it's often more interesting to work with the undulation.

A stone stairway cut into this steep hillside provides the homeowners with access to the base of their property (and a good workout).

Although located on a cliff overlooking the Pacific Ocean, this property's backyard was graded to make it nearly level.

A series of concrete retaining walls transformed a steep slope into usable space featuring patios and planting beds.

Design: R. M. Bradshaw & Associates

Rather than recontour this gentle to moderate slope, the homeowners chose to create drifts of wildflowers and other blossoming plants.

TO RESHAPE OR NOT?

Rather than reshape your terrain, you may opt to work with what you have, and simply plant the hillside and build circulation paths. Other than carving out a few steps here and there, you wouldn't have to undertake any real grading.

Grading is in order if your plan involves leveling areas or smoothing out undulating slopes. On hillsides that aren't too steep, it's fairly easy to do some kinds of recontouring—for example, creating a series of level planting beds or terraces (see pages 106–107). You can probably muscle your way through a small job with a shovel and a wheelbarrow. If a lot of soil has to be shifted, you'll probably need to call in a professional with earth-moving equipment. Remember, any major changes to a slope, such as flattening part of it for a swimming pool, should be undertaken only after consulting a soils engineer, landscape architect, or other landscaping professional.

CONTOUR LINES

A plot plan or other survey of your hillside property may contain squiggles called contour lines; these curving lines connect points of the same elevation. A number next to a contour line tells you its height above sea level or another known point (such as a corner boundary marker). Uniform spacing between the contour lines indicates a constant slope, while irregular spacing signifies rolling or uneven terrain.

You can look at a map of a property with contour lines and get a feel for the lay of the land (assuming the terrain hasn't been regraded since the map was made). The contour lines will also give you an idea of how the land drains; you can see where the high and low points are and where any gullies are located.

Brick retaining walls create level planting areas in a small front yard that once sloped down to the street.

FACTORS TO CONSIDER

Before modifying your hillside with plants or structures, consider how the slope will affect the landscape and how the landscape will affect the slope. Learn about the various microclimates on your hillside; some may be more favorable than others for certain garden elements. Plan your landscape to take advantage of positive features, such as pleasing views, and to mitigate problems, such as lack of privacy. It's also important to be aware of your slope's technical aspects, such as soil type and drainage capacity, as well as the extent of any soil erosion problems. Seemingly innocent grading, paving, or watering can trigger astonishingly serious results if undertaken without forethought.

MICROCLIMATES

Most properties have several microclimates—areas that are a little warmer or cooler, wetter or drier, or more or less windy than others. These variations are created by a combination of factors, including topography, sun, wind, and the location of the house and other structures. Well-chosen microclimates can make seating and outdoor activities more comfortable, and, in freeze-prone climates, keep susceptible plants a few degrees warmer in winter.

Hills and hollows account for a great many variations in climate; for that reason, sloping lots tend to have more microclimates than flat properties. The side of a hill is

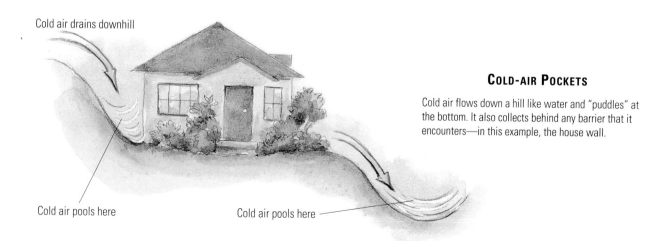

Cold air drains downhill

Cold air pools here

Cold air pools here

COLD-AIR POCKETS

Cold air flows down a hill like water and "puddles" at the bottom. It also collects behind any barrier that it encounters—in this example, the house wall.

warmer than the bottom because cold air flows downhill—though cold pockets can develop along the slope where a hedge, wall, or other obstacle impedes the airflow. The base of a hill or another cold pocket will also collect water. It's no place for garden seating or for plants that are frost-tender or that need hot, dry conditions—but it's a perfect spot for a bog garden.

The amount of sun that a site receives depends on its orientation. A site that faces north receives the least amount of sun, while a south-facing one gets the most. An east-facing site receives only morning sun, while a west-facing one gets the full force of the afternoon sun. Slopes intensify the solar effect. For example, a south-facing slope warms up very rapidly in spring; vegetables or flowers planted here get a jump on the season. A north-facing slope may be extremely shady; this exposure is too cool for seating in temperate climates but ideal in very hot ones.

Hilly terrain also intensifies the effects of wind. Exposed areas on peaks and hillsides tend to be buffeted by winds. Strong gusts may send you scurrying in from the patio, dry out plants, and snap tree limbs. If the problem is severe enough, you may want to install a windbreak to shelter the house and garden. Don't construct a solid wall; an impenetrable barrier simply deflects the wind briefly, then drops it back into the garden a few feet away. A better solution is to diffuse the wind with a closely spaced planting of fast-growing trees or shrubs placed perpendicular to the prevailing winds.

These succulents thrive on a warm, sunny slope.
Design: Harland Hand

VIEWS

Some hillside properties have vistas worth protecting or even designing a landscape around. If you're lucky enough to enjoy a panoramic view, don't block it. If ugly elements mar the outlook, mask them with plants or structures and frame any desirable scenes. If pleasing elements of faraway and near landscapes lie within your sight, as they often do in hilly areas, borrow the scenery for your composition: frame a distant rolling hillside from a lookout in your garden, and appropriate a neighbor's handsome grove of trees as a backdrop for your plantings.

On the other hand, your vista may be more restricted. The view from the patio and perhaps from the family room and kitchen may be directly into a steep slope. In that case, use landscaping elements that you will enjoy looking at all year—for example, plants with colorful evergreen foliage or deciduous plants that offer a progression of

Glass panels protect this patio from the full force of winds without sacrificing the panoramic view of the hills beyond.

Although far from secluded, this sloping backyard gains some sense of privacy from fences and plants along the property lines.

interest, such as delicate spring flowers, ornamental summer fruit, bright fall foliage, and a striking winter silhouette.

PRIVACY

The sensation of being in a goldfish bowl is familiar to people living on small lots where houses are set close together. The problem is usually exaggerated in hilly areas. Perhaps your property rises sharply above a neighboring lot, putting more of your neighbor's house and yard on display than you care to see. At the same time, your neighbor on the uphill side may loom over your property, making you uncomfortable every time you venture into your own yard.

Observe how your property lies in relation to adjoining lots and determine which sight lines can be blocked with strategically placed plants or with structures such as fences and trellises. You may not be able to seclude every part of your property, but you can create private retreats within the landscape.

SOIL TYPE

Having a general idea of your slope's soil characteristics is helpful before you start landscaping. Is the soil so loose and rocky or sandy that it tends to slide downhill? If so, you may have to shore up the slope with a retaining wall and sink deck supports extra deep. Or is your soil a heavy clay that's nearly impossible to dig? In that case, building terraced beds filled with improved soil may be better than trying to excavate individual planting holes on the hillside. Or is your soil a good loam? If it is, digging holes—for plants as well as fence posts—will be easy.

SOIL EROSION

Water from rainfall and melting snow courses downhill, taking soil with it and gradually eroding the slope. The problem is usually worse on ground that has been filled with soil excavated from another part of the slope, especially if it has not been adequately compressed.

Before your neighborhood was developed, chances are that most of the moisture was absorbed by the soil. Now roofs and paved surfaces collect the water that would have soaked in and concentrate it in small streams; the result is too much water moving across the terrain too quickly to infiltrate the soil. If water runs rampant across a property, it may start landslides, break down retaining walls, undermine house foundations, and convert patios into ponds.

If you're new to your property, try a simple test for a clue to how much water will run off during wet weather. Dig a hole of any width and about 2 feet deep; fill it with water. After it drains, fill it again. If it takes hours or even days to drain, you'll know that most of the water from heavy rainfalls or snowmelt will run off the surface. The steeper the slope, the more severe the runoff—and resulting erosion—will be.

Even if you don't see water washing away your soil, you can detect signs of erosion fairly easily. The most obvious indications are tree roots exposed above ground (except in species that grow that way naturally); small stones or rocks previously underground now on the ground surface; small gullies that have formed; silt or sediment built up in low areas or on pavement; soil splashed on outside walls; and stream channels that have widened or deepened. If you suspect a serious erosion problem on your property (or on a neighboring one that may affect yours), seek professional advice from a structural or soils engineer, an erosion control specialist, or an engineering geologist.

Any hillside that isn't completely covered with plants or structures will erode to some degree, so your landscape plan should address erosion control even if you don't see danger signs. Drainage systems, retaining walls, and terraces are all proven controls (see page 89). Plants are also effective in combating erosion (and they cost less than structures); see page 123 for a list of plants

An unplanted or sparsely planted slope is especially prone to soil erosion. There's nothing to stop wind from blowing away loose soil or to stop water running downhill from taking soil with it. A dense cover of plants will help preserve the slope.

whose dense or wide-spreading root systems make them good candidates for growing on hillsides.

Take care not to erode or destabilize the slope in the process of landscaping. For example, you may want to remove several trees from a shady slope to let in more light and make room for lower-growing plants. Instead of digging out the stumps and root systems, leave them in place to rot slowly. Or, if you're building a deck on a steep slope, be sure to sink the concrete footings sufficiently deep into the hillside (see page 109).

MEASURING YOUR SLOPE

You can often eyeball a slope and accurately determine whether it is suitable for a certain landscaping purpose, just as you can walk a proposed route to see whether steps are necessary. But at times you may need to measure elevation differences between various points or determine the grade of the slope (see below). If you're simply planting the hillside, there's usually no need to measure either elevations or grade.

Measuring elevation changes is helpful if you plan to terrace the slope or build structures such as stairways or fences that step down in level sections. If you plan to cut

MAKING THE GRADE

Calculating the grade—the relationship between the horizontal run and the vertical rise of your slope—can be useful when planning certain landscaping operations (such as cutting and filling) or features (such as lawns or paths) that have recommended minimum and maximum grades.

Grade is usually expressed as a ratio or percentage. The ratio tells you how many feet of horizontal run there are for every foot of vertical rise. If, over a 40-foot distance, a slope rises 8 feet, it has a slope ratio of 40:8, or 5:1. Percent of grade is the change in elevation over 100 feet; to determine this figure, divide the rise (8 feet) by the run (40 feet) and multiply by 100; in this case, the grade is 20 percent. A grade can exceed 100 percent if the slope's rise is greater than its length. The chart at right lists maximum and minimum grades for some common landscape elements.

SUITABLE GRADES

Slope ratio	Percent grade	Angle (approx.)	
1:1	100%	45°	Maximum for cut slopes
2:1	50%	27°	Maximum for fill slopes and ground covers
3:1	33%	18°	Maximum for simple construction
4:1	25%	14°	Maximum for lawn—hard to mow
5:1	20%	12°	Maximum for lawn—easy to mow
10:1	10%	6°	Maximum for paths and ramps
20:1	5%	3°	Maximum for "flat" surface
100:1	1%	1°	Looks flat; minimum for drainage

Landscapers will sometimes refer to a slope's angle of steepness; this figure tells you how much the slope deviates from the horizontal. For example, a hillside with a 1:1 slope ratio (which for every 1 foot of distance rises 1 foot) climbs upward at a 45-degree angle. You can often get a pretty good idea of the angle just by looking at the slope; however, a 100:1 slope, which rises at a 1-degree angle, is so slight that you can't detect it with your eye. The reason for measuring such a minuscule grade is that all landscaping surfaces should be sloped for drainage, and 1 percent is the minimum that landscape professionals use. The chart above lists the angle equivalent for each grade.

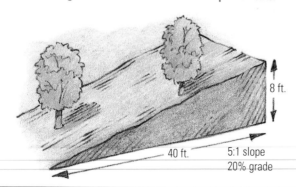

8 ft.

40 ft.　5:1 slope
20% grade

or fill soil, or to install lawns, paths, or other features with a recommended slope, you'll also probably want to measure the grade of the area where you'll be putting the feature.

You could rent a surveyor's level, or transit, but simpler, less expensive tools may be used if you don't require great precision. The methods described here will give you "good enough" measurements for most landscaping purposes. For short distances, a straight board, carpenter's level, and tape are adequate (see page 92). With a line level or hand level, you can more easily survey a longer slope. A line level allows you to measure the slope's grade as well as elevation differences; a hand level is good for determining elevations only. The various levels are sold at building centers and hardware stores.

LINE LEVEL

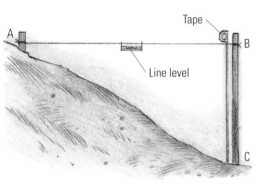

This is a small level that hooks onto a string line stretched taut between two points at different elevations (between A and C in the illustration at left). Hammer a short stake into the ground at the top (A) and a tall stake at the downhill point (C); keep the distance between the stakes to within 50 feet. Stretch mason's line between the two stakes; hang the level on the string and adjust the string until the bubble in the level is centered. At the tall stake, use a tape to measure the distance from the string to the ground (B to C); this distance represents the drop-off, or vertical rise, in the slope between the top and bottom stakes. To determine the horizontal run, measure along the string line (from A to B). For a long slope, repeat the measuring in stages down the slope; total the vertical distances for the drop-off, and the linear measurements for the horizontal run. To determine your slope's grade, see "Making the Grade" on the opposite page.

HAND LEVEL

This tool is like a small telescope but with a built-in level. It lets you determine the difference in elevation between where you're standing and a point farther along the slope where a helper has positioned an upright measuring rod. You can make a rod by marking foot and inch increments on a 12-foot-long 1 by 2 or scrap piece of lumber (if 12 feet isn't long enough for a steep slope, measure down the slope in intervals and total the drop-offs). As an alternative, you could use a wide steel tape, though it's hard to keep the tape vertical on a windy day.

Have your helper hold the rod upright at a reference point (such as a corner of the house). Standing erect, look through the hand level at the rod until the bubble is centered; record the rod measurement intersected by the bubble. This is the reference elevation. It also represents your eye level; take all subsequent readings in the same upright stance.

Take sitings of other points as necessary; the distance above or below the reference number equals the difference in elevation. Taking all measurements from one reference point is ideal, though not always possible. You may measure from several points as long as you reference them to each other; list the initial reference point as zero and record elevation differences in inches. You may also find it handy to pound stakes into the ground at the various points you've measured and record their elevations on the stakes.

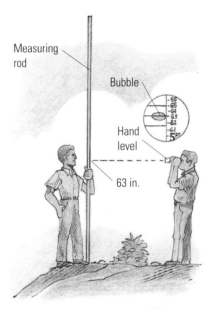

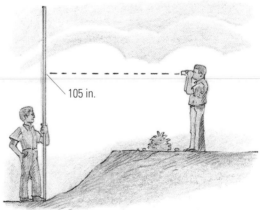

First, take a preliminary reading to determine your eye level in inches (top). Then, take a reading of the rod held at a point where you want to determine the elevation difference (bottom). Subtract the figure representing your eye level from the subsequent reading; in this example, 105 inches minus 63 inches equals 42 inches, or 3½ feet.

If you're looking for inspiration, this chapter is guaranteed to spark ideas. The following pages take you on a pictorial tour of beautiful hillside properties, arranged by landscape area

INSPIRING
IDEAS

or feature—front slopes, back slopes, steps and paths, retaining walls, decks, and so on. Whatever your ter-rain and surroundings, you'll find situations you can relate to. The slopes range from slight to steeply pitched, and the settings from spacious country properties to tight city lots.

Pay special attention to the hardscape materials. If you hadn't considered concrete because you thought it too sterile, observe how its appearance can be softened by plants. If you think stone is just stone, see how the colors, shapes, and arrange-ments vary and how much interest rock work can add to a gar-den. Notice the creative uses of wood, brick, and other materials in many of the gardens.

Rather than copy a landscape, use it as a springboard for your own ideas, to suit your needs and wants. Take note of the whimsical or individualistic details shown on these pages, and think about how you might inject your personality into a garden.

Retaining walls hold back this slope and form a backdrop for the swimming pool.
Design: Conni Cross and Carol Nelson

FRONT SLOPES

Because a streetside slope is on public view, it should make a favorable impression. But good looks alone aren't enough if the property slopes to any significant degree—any technical concerns, like erosion control, must also be satisfied. There are many ways to beautify a slope and protect it from slipping; the solutions presented on the following pages include rock gardens and planting terraces.

The handsome rock garden shown above stabilizes the nearly vertical bank between the sidewalk and a small lawn at the top of the slope. Large trees overhanging the front porch offer a sheltering welcome to visitors.

Rather than create a wall or screen for privacy, the owners of this corner property turned their front yard into a public spectacle. Their lavish rock garden features a wide variety of colorful plants, as well as boulders selected for their interesting contours. Uplights dotting the slope allow the homeowners—and passersby—to enjoy the display at night.

The cut and uncut stones in this retaining wall look as if they were casually piled, but they were meticulously stacked to achieve that effect. The stones were chosen for diverse shapes and for deep tones that harmonize with the dark brick of the house facade.

Building the stacked-stone retaining wall below allowed the homeowners to create a gently sloping garden area behind the wall. Plants spill over the top of the wall and from the crevices between rocks.

This low, dry-laid retaining wall of cut stones holds back a modest slope. Plants at the base of the wall soften the rock work; another colorful border behind the wall abuts a small lawn. A decorative arched arbor beckons visitors to the house.

Nestled among the trees, this home feels so private that the patio was placed off the front entrance. The lawn was planted on fairly flat terrain; mixed plantings cover the slope at left in the photo.

The Victorian house at right overlooks cut-stone terraces. The space behind each retaining wall was not leveled but gently sloped. The heavily mulched plantings easily hold the soil in place.

Design: Conni Cross

The stepping-stone path and stone-slab stairway leading to the house above are informal-looking, in keeping with the woodsy setting. The bench on the front porch is a snug spot to sit and admire nature.

Design: Conni Cross

This mountaintop home was built around natural rock ledges; the large outcropping seen at left serves as a focal point in the landscape. A bluestone walkway leads to the front entrance. The stone used in the retaining walls matches that in the house facade.

Design: Johnsen Landscapes and Pools

Designed to look wild, the landscape shown above contains a mix of annuals, perennials, and shrubs, including drought-tolerant Rocky Mountain natives. Many of the plants, such as poppies *(Papaver)* and violas, reseed freely.

Design: Great Gardens of Denver

Plants were set in neat rows for a pleasing horizontal pattern in the terraced hillside below. Vines mask a concrete retaining wall at the bottom of the property; a portion of a wooden retaining wall partway up the slope is visible at far right.

This short bank between the sidewalk and fence was transformed into an arresting rock garden. The dark boulders contrast nicely with the largely pastel tones of the plants.

The owners of this waterfront property succeeded beautifully in their goals to tame the hillside and create a gracious entrance to their home, which sits 100 feet below the street-level garage. The best of the wild plants, including all established trees, were saved and supplemented with cultivated stock. Retaining walls were built to shore up the slope, and a winding wooden walkway was installed. Pocket gardens, such as the miniature pool shown in the photo at right, provide interesting sights along the way.

Design: Henrikus Schraven

A bluestone walkway with steps between long ramps traverses the modest slope at left. A vibrant mixed border separates large patches of dwarf periwinkle *(Vinca minor)* in the foreground and lawn in front of the house.

Design: Ireland-Gannon

Pulling into this driveway is a pleasure because of the bright flora on either side. The plantings also divert attention from the driveway itself, which slopes rather awkwardly in two directions.

A colorful patchwork of low-maintenance perennials holds this bank between the driveway and house. Stepping-stones leading to the house zigzag across the slope rather than steeply descending it.

Design: Maile Arnold

BACK SLOPES

A backyard landscape is usually more personal than a streetside one, especially if the yard is concealed from public view. Even if somewhat exposed, the backyard is traditionally the domain of the homeowners, who can fill it with plants or string up hammocks as they see fit. Whatever you want for your back slope, remember to satisfy any requirements for drainage and erosion control.

The concrete-and-stone staircase seen above traverses a gentle slope retained by stacked stone walls. The greenhouse was conveniently located adjacent to the house on graded ground.

A rock garden featuring large, moss-covered boulders shores up the bank behind the house. Additional rocks and plantings were set along the edges of the wood-and-mulch stairs that descend the steep slope.

The heavily mulched slope planted with rhododendrons levels out to a lawn that is set apart from the hill by a wood edging. A stairway wends downhill through a tunnel of foliage.

The private hillside retreat at left features a comfortable bench and luxuriant plantings, including colorful ones in wooden planters on the decking and built into the bench back. A wooden retaining wall—which holds the slope above the staircase—steps up in level sections. A vine-covered arbor with a gate leads to another garden "room."

Slope-holding plants grow on either side of this curving log-and-mulch stairway, which leads to a flat space with planting beds dug into a lawn. The attractive arbored gate in the picket fence is a focal point.

Design: Conni Cross

The Southern California home shown above and at right has a steep backyard made accessible by a stairway that snakes up the hill. The slope plantings were chosen for erosion-controlling ability and fire resistance.

The sharp slope below is easily navigated thanks to the curving wood-and-gravel stairway; its simple design is in keeping with the informal plantings. A patio roof provides relief from the hot desert sun.

The terraced hillside above contains a series of zigzagging staircases and small decks, all bounded by steel railings for safety. Drought-tolerant vegetation, including ivy *(Hedera)* and ornamental grasses, colors the slope.

Design: Michael Moshier

The wood-and-aggregate stairway shown above permits close-up viewing of the wide range of flora chosen for their diverse forms and colors. A pool edged by mortared stone paving sits at the base of the stairs.

Unthirsty, slope-holding plants form a tapestry of green and yellow, with touches of blue and rosy pink, on the hillside above. This planting uses rocks sparingly as accents.

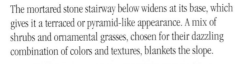

The mortared stone stairway below widens at its base, which gives it a terraced or pyramid-like appearance. A mix of shrubs and ornamental grasses, chosen for their dazzling combination of colors and textures, blankets the slope.

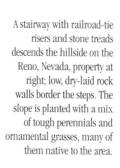

A stairway with railroad-tie risers and stone treads descends the hillside on the Reno, Nevada, property at right; low, dry-laid rock walls border the steps. The slope is planted with a mix of tough perennials and ornamental grasses, many of them native to the area.

The landscape shown above illustrates the genius of working with nature. Here, a mix of shade-loving, woodland plants looks perfectly at home in the woodsy setting.

The low-growing perennials covering the northern Colorado slope below echo the wildflower fields of the surrounding Rocky Mountains—although this planting isn't limited just to natives.

Design: Lauren Springer

A colorful meadow like the one above is simple and unpretentious, but it's anything but plain—it covers this gently sloping terrain like a beautiful quilt. Using native plants, especially ones that reseed, increases the likelihood of a good show every year.

A vivid patch of pink-flowering ice plant decorates the slope of this property overlooking the Pacific Ocean. In such a setting, plantings should be erosion controlling as well as wind- and salt-tolerant.

The backyard of the modestly sloping Iowa property shown below contains an eye-popping swath of prairie wildflowers featuring black-eyed Susan *(Rudbeckia hirta)*.

DECKS

A well-designed deck transforms sloping, sometimes unusable land into level space on which to lounge, entertain, dine, or otherwise enjoy outdoor living. The deck that works best for you may be a single-level structure that hovers above the landscape or a multi-level one that descends into it. You may decide on a basic rectangular deck or a more elaborate, angled or curved deck with built-in benches and planters.

On the woodsy property above and at right, the deck spans the width of the house, then steps down to a runway leading to an additional seating area nestled among the trees and shrubbery. The entire deck, extension and all, seems to float.

This freestanding deck partway down a steep slope was strategically located for optimum viewing of the surrounding countryside and to take advantage of light shade beneath several oak trees.

LEFT: These custom railings with rows of steel cable and turnbuckles are not only attractive but also barely visible, so they don't block the spectacular view.

BOTTOM: Several levels of decks wrap around the house, providing the homeowners with different views. The decks were constructed to look like integral parts of the house rather than add-ons.

Design (left): Mark Meryash

ABOVE: This deck built over a foggy valley features a built-in bench that can seat lots of guests.

RIGHT: Cantilevered over a steep, woodsy hillside and designed to accommodate several mature trees, this deck has the feel of a tree house.

Design (above): Royston, Hanamoto, Alley & Abey, Landscape Architects

Design (right): Tramontano & Rowe

This multitiered waterfront deck steps down to the water in stages, following the slope. The design allows an unobstructed view of the lake from inside the house.

LEFT: A multilevel deck transformed a steep hillside into a spacious outdoor room. The deck features spot lighting and built-in benches with seat backs that double as planters.

ABOVE: Hillside properties often contain little space for child's play. Here, the upper level of a large, multilevel deck provides plenty of room for fun and games. The lower tier is a restful area for contemplating nature (for an additional view, see page 29, bottom right).

Design (left): John Montgomery/Garden Architecture

Design (above): Tramontano & Rowe

The homeowners opted for a low deck rather than a patio on the barely sloping area overlooking a moderate hillside. The freeform structure features a modest change of levels and built-in seating. A cutout in the deck accommodates a large tree.

Design: Ireland-Gannon

Good lighting is essential for safe use of a multilevel deck at night. Light sensors turn on these deck light fixtures at dusk.

ABOVE: People relaxing on the upper deck can stay high and dry, away from splashes that wet the ground-level pool deck.

RIGHT: A path leads to this secluded, stand-alone deck featuring a clematis-covered arbor.

Design (above): Johnsen Landscapes and Pools

The narrow, squiggly-edged deck above and at right was designed to fit snugly into a natural rock ledge in the hillside. The ledge was turned into a rock garden that adds visual appeal to the deck area; many of the tiny rock garden plants are meant to be viewed close-up.

Design: Johnsen Landscapes and Pools

LEFT: A cascade of stairs and landings pinwheels around a rock outcropping and two mature trees. The freestanding stairs that lead down from the upper-level deck are supported by cross-stacked 4 by 4s.

BELOW: A curving edge allowed close fitting of the deck around existing plants.

Design (left): Scott Padgett

This deck features various widths of floorboards arranged in a random pattern and a wooden privacy screen. Where slopes are hard to navigate, as they are on this property, desktop containers bring garden sights and fragrances close-up.

Wooden planter boxes built onto the outside edge of the deck, as well as pots on the deck surface, provide extra growing space on a steep hillside lot. If container plantings are numerous, you may want to consider an automatic drip system to ease watering chores.

Wicker seating and rustic tables give this arbored deck the feel of a living room. The overhead structure provides a place to train vines; even uncovered, the arbor will cast shadows that provide some relief from direct sun.

Design: Landscape Environments Ltd.

PATIOS AND SITTING PLACES

A patio can be a perfect lounging spot on any part of your property that is flat or easily flattened. For dining and entertaining, a patio near the house is most convenient; a remote patio serves better as a quiet retreat. You'll appreciate additional sitting places where there's a good view or where you need to rest while navigating your hillside. Set out garden chairs or benches or use more informal seating, like flat-topped boulders.

ABOVE: This shady, very private brick patio is located on level ground between the house and the terraced hillside. A drainage system is essential to carry away water flowing down the slope.

BELOW: Seeded aggregate—created by embedding colorful pebbles and stones in concrete—teams with brick in this spacious patio. Matching brickwork is used in the retaining walls and planters.

Design (below): Curtis Gelotte Architects

Timber edgings hold bricks in place in the multi-level patio below. A wood insert laid in the brick accommodates an existing tree. The wrought-iron bench encircling the tree protects the trunk and provides additional seating.

Design: Goldberg & Rodler

A deck may be the obvious choice to overlook a steep streetside slope, but the homeowners of this property decided on a cantilevered patio. The semicircular, limestone-lined entertainment patio, which sits well above neighboring rooftops, features its own cooking center and access to the kitchen through double-wide French doors.

Design: Van-Martin Rowe Design of Pasadena

This wedge of patio takes advantage of available level space between the house and hillside. A geometric design of cast-concrete slabs forms the patio floor; grass is planted between the rectangles.

Design: Studio 6 Design

Several shades of cut bluestone in various sizes of rectangles and squares blend beautifully in the floor of the elevated patio shown above; the stones were tightly laid without mortar. Fieldstone walls give a sense of comforting enclosure to the patio.

Design: Johnsen Landscapes and Pools

A geometric pattern of concrete pavers sits on an easy-draining base of packed gravel. Pressure-treated wood edgings help lock the patio in place. Built-in benches provide seating that may be supplemented by movable patio furniture.

Design: Lankford Associates

This freeform flagstone patio on a woodsy hillside terrace is really nothing more than an expanded path connecting two stairways. The irregularly shaped flagstones were arranged like a giant jigsaw puzzle and set directly in soil. On the uphill side, the patio is bounded by a curving stone retaining wall, one of several on the hillside.

What can you do with a steep slope on a small urban lot? On the property shown below and at left, the slope was built up to make space for a front-yard patio with great views. A new concrete-block retaining wall was constructed on top of the existing one (below), then backfilled and dressed with concrete pavers, trellised railings, built-in benches, and a sunny garden bed (at left).

Design: Lankford Associates

This pink-tinted concrete-slab patio was built on flat terrain between two terraced retaining walls—a stone retaining wall on the uphill side and a concrete block one supporting the slab. Plants at the edges of the patio soften the look of the concrete.

A compact patio serves as a rest stop between two stairways on a hillside lot. Large concrete pavers form an attractive, stable floor.

On this Ketchum, Idaho, property, Montana slate was chosen for the patio floor and local quartzite for the steps and built-in bench. Instead of mortar, creeping perennials fill the cracks between the stones.

Two nearby seating areas are paved with gravel and bounded by fieldstones. Adirondack chairs give the space behind the house the feel of a full-fledged patio, while the garden bench tucked into the edge of the curving pathway makes for a more informal relaxation place.

A log-and-mulch stairway leads to a bench nestled in shrubbery and shaded by tall trees. Although adjacent to the house, the resting spot feels secluded enough for quiet contemplation.

Design: Conni Cross

Flagstones form the seat of this bench built into the corner of a stone retaining wall. The heart-shaped stone fragment in the seat back provides a touch of whimsy.

Design: Lucy Hardiman

This remote retreat on an east-facing hillside is a choice spot for viewing sunrises. The sturdy arbor rises above a floor of flagstones set in soil, with low creepers planted in the crevices between the stones.

Design: Lankford Associates

Placed at the top of a bluestone stairway, the Adirondack chair is an irresistible lure to anyone wanting to rest and admire the view.

Design: Lisa Stamm, Landscape Architect

Sitting places can go anywhere you want them. This wooden bench was tucked into a shady spot in front of a rock garden.

Flagstones and small creeping plants make up the floor of this level platform created by a dry-laid stone retaining wall and back-filled, compressed soil. The bench is an agreeable spot for viewing the garden below; fragrant roses entice sitters to stay longer.

STEPS AND PATHS

People tend to enjoy their gardens more if they can get around them easily. Being able to navigate safely is important, too, especially on slopes. On a gentle incline, slip-resistant paths may suffice as passageways—but the steeper the terrain, the greater the need to incorporate steps in the paths. Luckily, there's no need to forfeit beauty for safety, as is evident from the attractive, often innovative solutions shown on the following pages.

A wide staircase fashioned from thick stone slabs makes a bold statement. Some of the joints were left unmortared for use as planting pockets. Additional slabs stacked at the edges of the passageway serve as retaining walls.

ABOVE: Diminutive ground covers creep from the joints between basalt slabs, embellishing the stones without overrunning them.

LEFT: Immense sandstone slabs form a handsome, solid stairway. The variation in slab width creates a pleasing staggered effect.

Design (above): Robert W. Chittock & Associates

Design (left): Conni Cross and Susan Roth

The stone staircase at left gracefully curves to fit the slope. Plants growing in pockets at the edges and back of each tread spill onto the steps.

Fairly thin stones were stacked to achieve the desired riser height in the staircase above. A landing encourages visitors to stop and enjoy the lush plantings. Lighting fixtures located along the stairs are essential for nighttime safety.

ABOVE: Thick stone steps with succulents growing in the joints terminate in two stones pieced like an arrowhead, pointing the way to a path.

RIGHT: Stones in this mortared staircase are tan, light brown, and cream— a beautiful contrast with the charcoal gray of the stacked rock wall.

Design (right): Bob Clark

The very simple stairway shown below climbs a shallow slope through an herb garden. The risers are made of staked dimensional lumber; the treads consist of a generous layer of mulch on top of compressed soil.

A railroad-tie staircase leads to an ornate gazebo in a surprising but successful marriage of informal and formal. Low, creeping plants fill the tread space, softening the look of the steps.

In this Asian-inspired garden, a Japanese maple *(Acer palmatum)* accents a curving stairway featuring wooden pole risers and mulch treads. The colors of the wood and mulch harmonize with tones in the stacked rock wall.

Design: Portland International Garden & Design

The wooden steps at right bring to mind ladders laid against a slope. The open risers are filled with stones to visually tie the stairway to the rock garden it traverses. The stone filling also acts as a mulch, neatening the space below the steps and keeping down weeds.

A neatly constructed railroad-tie stairway was incorporated into a low retaining wall of the same material. The steps lead to wooden decking around a swimming pool.

This wooden passage reminiscent of a seaside boardwalk loops through plantings and steps down to a beach below.

Design: Randolf Marshall, Landscape Architect

Low ground covers give the extra-wide aggregate steps shown above the look of planting terraces. The plants are set in 3½-inch-wide pockets in front of each riser.

Design: Robert W. Chittock & Associates

LEFT: The risers in this stairway are broken pieces of an old concrete-slab patio; gravel loosely fills the tread spaces. Decorative river rocks are strewn along the edges.

ABOVE: Each step of this poured concrete staircase was rounded at the lip for a softer look, and the concrete was tinted steel gray to harmonize with the stacked rock walls. The metal handrail makes angular turns rather than following the curve of the stairs, for a pleasing contrast.

Design (left): Richard William Wogisch

Design (above): Michael Moshier

Concrete steps can be cast in any shape for which you can construct a form. In the stairway at left, round slabs are overlapped.

Potted plants draw attention away from the starkness of the poured concrete stairway shown below. Wood edgings for the in-ground plantings butt up against the steps.

In the front walkway pictured above, aggregate steps zigzag around planting spaces filled with lavender. The stairway's predictability—sequences of two steps followed by a landing—makes tripping less likely.

The curved staircase and low retaining walls at right are made of artificial cast stone. The construction process involves forming a shell of reinforcing bar and wire mesh, then covering it in layers of concrete. The "stone" is then sculpted to mimic the real thing.

Tile is a common material in Mediterranean gardens such as the one shown above. Terra-cotta tiles matching those of the patio floor are used on the stair treads, while two patterns of feature tiles appear on alternate risers.

Rather than repeat the stonework of the steps, the builder of the mortared stone stairway shown below turned the landing into a work of art by piecing together stone and tile fragments in a mosaic pattern.

In the mortared brick stairs shown below, the lower bricks in each riser were set on end and the upper ones horizontally to achieve the desired riser height. Plants spilling onto the steps give the impression of staggered tread widths.

A stairway made of timber risers and unmortared brick treads cuts a path through a series of landscape timber retaining walls. In their route, the steps illustrate a successful union of angles and curves.

A gravel path doesn't need any steps on a gentle slope such as the one shown above. Be prepared to add more gravel periodically, as some will slide downhill over time—and spread sideways, too, if there is no edging.

Fairly level ground was dug out of this hillside for a lightly graveled path. A stone retaining wall holds the slope on the uphill side. A stone border on the downhill side retains the gravel.

A gravel path encircles a knot garden of dwarf boxwood twisting around pink astilbe and ends at a cast-concrete model of winged Nike, the Greek goddess of victory. Three sizes of gravel were used to prevent any shifting beneath one's feet: 1 inch for the base; then finely crushed, to filter down between the large pieces; and pea size on top.

The boulder stepping-stone path pictured below meanders through colorful plantings that spill onto the path and creep into the joints between the closely spaced stones.

The concrete stepping-stones shown above were cast on site; each was individually molded and carved to mimic genuine stone. The "boulders" flanking the path were constructed in the same way.

Design: Harland Hand

The stepping-stones above traverse a gently sloping shade garden, pictured in winter with a pine needle mulch and and a dusting of snow.

When a beautiful garden beckons, the call may go unheeded if touring is difficult. Here, it couldn't be easier—the journey begins at steps connecting the deck with a flagstone path leading to a wooden footbridge over a stream.

Design: Johnsen Landscapes and Pools

This mortared walkway of various-colored flagstones edged with brick takes a pleasing serpentine path down a shallow slope. Because the curving descent is gradual, steps are unnecessary.

Design: Bob Clark

ABOVE: On this terraced hillside, a decomposed granite path is edged by a railroad-tie retaining wall on the uphill side and benderboard on the downhill side. On a lower terrace, a swath of grass serves as a path.

BELOW: A side view of this garden shows one of a series of grass paths traversing the slope between planting beds. When the landscape is viewed from the top or bottom of the hill, the paths are invisible.

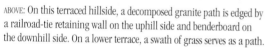

Stepping-stones through a lawn lead to a mortared brick path along another patch of turf. The elevation difference is great enough to warrant two steps—a sloping brick walk would be too slippery in rainy or icy weather.

Steps and Paths **49**

RETAINING WALLS

This type of wall has tough demands on it—hold back a slope, support leveled ground behind it for planting or building on, and help prevent soil erosion— but with just the right design and materials for the situation, it can succeed beautifully. On steeper hillsides, retaining walls are often indispensable for reclaiming unusable space. Even on gentle inclines where they may not be absolutely necessary, they're popular as design elements.

The pattern of the block-shaped cut stones in this dry-laid, low wall mimics the ashlar masonry in the house facade. The gracefully curving wall looks almost like a decorative ribbon running the length of the perennial border.

ABOVE: Pieces of limestone—surprisingly heavy for their thin shape— were stacked on top of each other to form a handsome retaining wall. Using slender slabs like these leaves no large gaps that have to be filled.

LEFT: The large stones in this dry-laid wall were carefully fitted for tight joints. Gaps were filled with smaller stones and stone fragments.

Design (left): Roger Warner

The low wall at right has loose joints that are thickly mortared. Weep holes—pieces of pipe for funneling water through the wall—were set in the mortar at regular intervals; one is visible protruding through a joint in the lower tier.

The fieldstone wall shown above has fairly tight joints—and much less mortar showing than in the wall at top right of this page. Prominence of mortar is a style decision more than anything else.

You can plant in front of and behind a retaining wall—and with a dry-laid wall like this one, you can also set small plant species in the crannies between stones. Many of the crevice plantings shown here are succulents, which thrive with the good drainage and air circulation they receive in the wall's gaps.

This riprap wall was easily built by placing fieldstones of various sizes directly against the shallow bank. The rocks not only help keep the slope from eroding, but they also make a tidy border for the driveway.

Two enormous stone slabs form the seat and backrest of the bench built into this dry-stacked stone wall. All the stones in the wall were painstakingly chosen for pleasing shape and color.

Design: Sandra Wendel

Weathered railroad ties held together by metal straps nailed to the wood form a low wall at the property's frontage. The ties are repeated in a stairway leading to the front entrance. Bright annuals at the edges of both the wall and the steps offer relief from the brown color of the ties and large expanse of mulch.

This unusual retaining wall with an undulating top is made of landscape timbers cut to different lengths and positioned vertically. For stability, two-thirds of each timber in such a wall should be set below ground.

For the neatly constructed retaining wall shown at right, landscape timbers were laid down in an overlapping pattern to provide added strength at the corner joints. Incorporating a stairway of dimensional lumber rather than stone or other material created a unified look.

The projections in this landscape timber wall are "deadmen" — timbers inserted at right angles to the wall surface and extending back into the slope for the purpose of tying the wall more securely to the hillside.

This rustic retaining wall consists of layers of thick logs. Cut lengths of narrower logs inserted into the ground in front of the wall and secured to it are used as supports, in the same way that 4-by-4 posts bolster a board wall.

Design: Robert W. Chittock & Associates

Intentionally crooked tiers with some bricks jutting out randomly give this retaining wall an intriguing eccentricity. Two planters built into the bottom of the wall provide extra growing space.

Design: Bob Clark

This steep Seattle lot previously covered in ivy was rebuilt after it slipped in torrential rains; terraced retaining walls now hold the rear slope securely. The bottom wall is concrete block veneered with brick to match the patio and walkway. The upper two walls are made of heavy-duty modular concrete blocks with a stonelike surface; they are anchored by a reinforcing geotextile fabric set deep in the hillside. All the construction work was done by hand because the lot is wedged into a gully where there is no way to bring in earth-moving equipment.

Design: Nakano Associates

Low retaining walls in the lawn and taller ones in front of the house step down neatly in sections. All are made of brick to match the house facade. Wiring for the light fixtures was hidden inside the walls during construction.

A repetition of materials—brick in the stepped retaining wall and in the fence posts—helps unify the garden. The wide cap on the wall is a good resting spot for potted plants, and people, too.

The walls in the photos above and below left are made of split-face concrete blocks, a rough-surface type of block fabricated to resemble cut stone. In both situations, a decorative cap completes the elegant look. Plants spilling over the walls and planted in front of them add an extra decorative dimension.

Retaining walls made of modular concrete blocks that lock together are among the easiest types for the do-it-yourselfer to build, yet they do a good job of restraining slopes. Styles vary; the blocks used in the walls shown above have a very manufactured appearance.

A steep hillside with a natural rock outcropping is a choice location for a waterfall. In the example below, water rushes down a curving channel worn in the rock formation. The water would flow on its own during rainy periods; pumping the water back to the top permits year-round enjoyment.

A picturesque koi pond fed by a small waterfall is the focal point in this sloping, small-space garden. A stone slab (bearing a wrought-iron chair in the photo) serves as a footbridge over the waterfall. Lush plantings mask the edges of the pond.

Below, Korean grass *(Zoysia tenuifolia)* forms sinuous, velvety hummocks among the artistically arranged stones flanking the waterfall. A line of stones placed in the path of the falling water deflects the force of the water entering the pond. A walkway provides access to the water's edge.

Just above the lowest spill stone in these falls is a shallow pool encircled by stacked rocks. When enough water collects there, the overflow drops into the pond. The irregular, jagged edge of the bottom spill stone produces widely spaced streams of water.

There's no more peaceful spot to contemplate the beauty of the pond and adjoining stream shown above than the waterfront bench. Built from stacked stone slabs, the bench doubles as a retaining wall.

The unusual pond shown above and at left is edged and studded with granite boulders. The cascading waterfall (at left) feeds the pond, which borders—and seems to flow into—the patio. Evergreen plantings soften the rock work and provide year-round interest.

Design: Robert W. Chittock & Associates

Stone slabs outline this small, freeform pond located on a plateau at the base of a rock outcropping. Natural rock ledges dot the slope below the pond.

The spill fountain at left was incorporated into tiered wooden planting beds built at the edge of an arbor. Water makes a pleasing splash as it pours from the carved lion's head into the low trough. To seal wood so it won't leak, coat it with asphalt emulsion or epoxy paint, or use a flexible liner.

The ornamental pool at right is built into the corner of the patio; its dark blue tiles and colorful, contrasting feature tiles harmonize beautifully with the patio's light blue concrete pavers. This small-space garden has room for another water feature—a birdbath—visible in the background.

Not all the raised beds in the garden below are devoted to plants growing in soil. The two terraced beds in the center foreground are water gardens filled with aquatic plants. Gravel paths incorporating timber-and-gravel steps wind through the garden.

Water bubbles up through the top of the metal sculpture in the pool above, filling the garden with soothing sounds. The pool's brickwork pattern echoes that of the terraced planting beds in the background.

Design: Bob Clark

Stones of different colors and sizes were used to create realistic and attractive dry creekbeds in the two gardens shown below. The creekbed at top runs under a stone-slab bridge and follows a gentle slope downhill. The one at bottom is located in a gully near the house and intercepts runoff from uphill.

Design (top): Robert W. Chittock & Associates

Some swimming pools feature expansive areas of paving and other hardscape without much in the way of plants to soften the hard edges. The pool shown above has a comfortable but not overlarge relaxation area—and it's surrounded by beautiful roses and other lush plantings.

Starting at the edge of the dichondra lawn, log terraces climb this slope. Metal stakes driven into the soil in front of the terraces hold the logs in place.

Very low walls incorporating both dimensional lumber and landscape timbers turned a shallow bank into level planting tiers for roses. Concrete stepping-stones are used as treads in steps up the bank.

LEFT: Railroad ties transformed a steep hillside into a terraced succulent garden; plants were set in the asymmetrically arranged raised beds and in the stairway treads. A dark stain gives the old, weathered ties a new look.

ABOVE: This rather formal planting of herbs grows in terraced beds made of landscape timbers; the tapered ends give the walls a distinctive look. The beds were stained to match the color of the adjoining deck and to unify the two structures.

Design (above): Designs of Mann

In these terraces the bricks in the lower tiers were set horizontally and capped, then another course of bricks was laid vertically and capped. The protruding lower cap has the effect of an ornamental border or chair rail. The terraces hold richly colored spring plantings, including tulips and nemesia. The brick is repeated in the entry walkway.

Design: Bob Clark

A varied brick pattern adds to the artistic appeal of these terraces. In the lower wall the bricks were set diagonally, while in the short upper walls they were placed horizontally.

ABOVE: A low concrete-block wall with a brick cap forms the bottom terrace on this shallow bank. Stacks of concrete pieces form additional tiers uphill.

RIGHT: This unconventional garden emphasizes hardscape rather than plants. The bricks, tiles, concrete pavers, and pieces of broken concrete in the terraces were stacked irregularly for an intentionally funky appearance; an unusual water feature at bottom right adds to the effect.

On this property, concrete pieces were neatly stacked into terraced walls. Those running across the slope have just enough room between the tiers for shallow plantings. The continuous wall descending the slope steps down in even sections.

Broken pieces of concrete are often used to build terraces, but they are typically laid flat; these were set on end for a novel look. The uneven heights of the pieces make the construction even more unusual.

ABOVE: Tiered planting beds were made of stucco to match the stairway and house walls. The planters hold colorful petunias.

LEFT: Concrete block walls support level planting beds for roses. The walls can be painted, as the lower one is, or left natural, like the upper one.

LAWN ON THE LEVEL

A lawn is more easily mowed and more efficiently watered when it's on fairly flat ground. If your land slopes or rolls too much for easy-to-tend turf, regrade a portion of it. Create a single level area or two or more tiers connected by steps and retaining walls.

ABOVE: A bold, mortared-stone retaining wall and stairway divide the upper lawn from the lower one. The top turf area serves as a patio, while the bottom one features attractive border plantings.

BELOW: A low, unmortared stone wall emphasizes the separation between the spacious lawn and the vibrant mixed border.

The two tiers of lawn are linked by stone-slab steps and a low stone wall that is obscured by the colorful planting of perennials and low shrubs.

Design: Barbara Martin

Dramatic circles of lawn descend in stair-step fashion down a moderate slope. The view at left shows a seating area partway down the slope; the stones in the foreground are steps from an upper grassy circle. The view below shows how the wide stone steps serve as retaining walls. The elevation change between the circles increases farther up the slope, as evidenced by the greater number of steps between tiers.

Design: Michael Schultz

The broad steps featuring brick risers and turf treads shown below link two levels of lawn. Brick is also used in the stairway edging and low retaining wall.

Brick walkways and steps combine with curving stone walls to create separate, bilevel garden "rooms," each dominated by lawn. The symmetrical arrangement of hardscape imparts a feeling of formality.

Design: Duncan Callicot

ROCK GARDENS

Hillsides and rock gardens were made for each other. Rocks offer an easy and convenient way to organize space on a slope, whether you take advantage of rock out-croppings or supply your own stones to make up for nature's lack. You needn't choose from classic rock garden plants; select any plants that please you and suit the surroundings.

The owner of this steep property capitalized on a natural rock ledge to create an unusual backyard rock garden featuring heaths *(Erica)* and heathers *(Calluna vulgaris).*

For this gently sloping rockery, the boulders as well as the shrubs, perennials, and ornamental grasses were chosen for their low profile.

A curving rock garden on the slope between the house and a level lawn features well-placed large boulders and smaller stones. A mulched path through the garden allows for easy maintenance of the various shrubs, perennials, and bulbs.

ABOVE: This rockery occupies a large triangular band between two level lawns. Gravel is used as a fast-draining mulch between the plants as well as a decorative border. Plants spilling over the low retaining wall and others planted in the gravel border ease the transition to lawn.

BELOW: Rocks rule on this steep slope. They were carefully chosen for color and shape, then spaced close together, with just enough room for plants to be tucked into the crevices between them.

When choosing rocks, look for some with indentations to hold water for wildlife. Here, a bird pauses to drink from dimpled moss rocks.

Design: Conni Cross

CONTAINER GARDENS

What do you do when planting space on a hillside is limited or hard to get to, or when steps, patios, or other hard surfaces look stark? The solution is simple. Just trot out an array of containers, fill them with colorful plants, and set them on any available level surface. For a continuing show, change plantings with the seasons.

These stone steps along a main walkway were built extra wide to showcase a collection of potted plants without impeding foot traffic.

Potted plants placed at the edges of the wooden stairway and on the hillside add most of the color and interest in this steep side yard. Containers range from fairly small clay pots to half-barrels.

Brightly hued plantings in decorative pots beautify a concrete patio. Setting pots on the sculptural pedestal (in right foreground) and on the artistically stacked brick wall puts some plant color at eye level.

Containers of tuberous begonias brighten a concrete stairway and a stacked rock wall. Just two or three small pots of colorful plants can create great visual interest.

Some plants may be difficult to grow or even see on a steep hillside, but you can enjoy them close-up on a deck. This grouping features lilies and oxalis.

On a hilly lot without much planting space, a flat-topped garage offers room for spectacular seasonal displays; the tulips will soon give way to summer-blooming plants. A drip line carries irrigation water to the wooden planter.

Whether you're creating a new garden or renovating an existing one, careful planning will help you create the kind of outdoor space you've always wanted. A well-thought-out landscape has a satisfying quality and an overall cohesiveness— attributes usually lacking in a space that is composed piecemeal or driven by impulse plant purchases.

IT'S ALL IN THE

PLANNING

You have a host of choices to make when planning a garden. Will you give top billing to plants because you're a gardener at heart? Or will you emphasize "hardscape"— landscape architects' term for hard surfaces such as patios, decks, walls, and walkways—because you'd rather recline on a chaise longue than putter with plants? Or will you strike a balance? Which plants will you choose? Which structures? Which paving materials?

If you don't know where to start or if the sheer number of possibilities immobilizes you, the methodical approach described in this chapter will move you in the right direction. Although you don't have to plan on paper, doing so will give you a sense of order and encourage you to think through every step. Working out your ideas on paper may also keep you from making costly mistakes.

In this three-tiered backyard, the deck steps down to a lawn, which steps down to a gravel path and planting area. Perennial and shrub borders along the yard's perimeter and a koi pond add to the serene mood.

Perennials, shrubs, and trees blanketing the front hillside combine forces with a short fence at the top to create a sense of privacy for the homeowners. The fence, which harmonizes with the house, forms one wall of an entry courtyard.

This landscape takes advantage of natural resources: rock outcroppings and smaller stones unearthed on the property. The stone steps lead to limestone ledges in the adjacent woods.

Design: Big Red Sun

SETTING GOALS

Even though the contours of your hillside may hint at certain landscaping features—as a gully might suggest a dry creekbed or a slope call to mind a series of framed terraces—forget about the terrain for the moment. The first step in planning any landscape, flat or hilly, is to decide what you want from it. Make a list of your landscaping goals and the ways you could fulfill them. Remember, both the goals and the interpretations are up to you. Try to be as specific and detailed as possible rather than broadly stating that your aim is, say, to create a beautiful setting for the house.

You'll find that well-defined goals suggest landscaping elements. For example, your goals may be to create privacy from neighboring properties, give the house more "street appeal," mask traffic noise, have a place for entertainment and relaxation, grow your own herbs and vegetables, and have a ready supply of flowers for bouquets. Those goals could translate into fences along the property lines, a handsome streetside rock garden, a bubbling fountain, a spacious patio, and terraced beds for edibles and cut flowers. Alternatively, they could translate into trees and tall shrubs along the boundaries, a dry-laid stone retaining wall and mixed plantings in the front yard, a waterfall, and a multilevel deck with built-in containers for edibles and flowers. Other interpretations depend on your tastes and preferences.

If another goal is to take advantage of your slope, the stone retaining wall, terraced beds, waterfall, and multilevel deck mentioned above are various ways to satisfy that objective. You may decide that the dry creekbed that originally came to mind is another good way to work with what you have, especially since it appeals to you. Don't include a feature simply because it fulfills a goal; you should be partial to it, because you'll live with it every day.

Don't forget to list your more mundane objectives—such as finding an inconspicuous spot for trash cans and keeping water from pooling on the garage floor during heavy rains. You can achieve those ends with an accessible, out-of-view service area and a drainage system to intercept water flowing toward the garage.

Your list is just the starting point; now you must reconcile it with your budget. You may have to get cost estimates for some of the features you have in mind to see if you're in the ballpark, or it may be clear right

Hard surfaces—steps, patios, benches, and planters—are featured in this graded landscape, while plants play a secondary role.

Design: Richard Bergmann, Architects

Colorful perennials and shrubs are the premier players in this plant lover's garden. They are set directly into the hillside and not into framed terraces or other structures.

away that you must scale back. If your ideas are bigger than your bank account, prioritize your goals and try to satisfy only the most important ones. Alternatively, find ways to implement all or most of them more modestly. For instance, if a dozen terraced planting beds would blow your budget, cut down on the number or plant directly in the hillside.

Even if cost is no obstacle, you must consider the amount of upkeep that your landscape will require, especially if you intend to do the work yourself. To reduce the amount of time and effort needed, avoid high-maintenance features such as lawns, sheared hedges, and flower beds.

Make as many refinements as needed until you're comfortable with the list you've compiled. Remember, your goals are paramount, but leave yourself open to modifying or completely changing your interpretations of them as you develop your plan.

MAKING CHOICES

Now is the time to make some decisions about your landscape. Think about the style of garden you want, and peruse the "ABC's of Garden Design" (see page 84) for ideas on how best to deal with your space. Reconsider your landscaping goals to be sure they're still on target. Also decide whether you really want to plan the garden on your own or to enlist help.

Regardless of who ends up doing the design, it's a good idea to compile a folder of garden ideas. Take photographs of gardens you like. Comb magazines and books for pictures of pleasing landscapes, flower beds, decks, fences, specimen plants—anything and everything that appeals to you.

A whimsical potting shed, with shelves to accommodate a collection of potted plants, expresses the owner's personality.

SELECTING A STYLE

You don't have to create a landscape with an obvious, identifiable theme, such as a Japanese garden or a native garden, but you should think about the general style of garden you'd like. Also consider ways of injecting your personal style into the landscape.

You might choose a garden style that reflects your region's climate: a desert

Carefully arranged gravel and stones—including tall, vertical ones—are among the hallmarks of Japanese-style gardens.

Strong symmetry identifies the landscape above right as formal, even though the walls flanking the stairway are curving rather than straight. In strictly formal gardens, prominent features are often arranged along an axis; notice that the pool, stairway, and fountain in this garden all line up. The landscape above is decidedly informal: a colorful mélange of plants shares a rolling hillside with randomly placed boulders, meandering paths, and a rustic arbor.

landscape in the arid Southwest, a tropical garden in southern Florida, or a Mediterranean garden in coastal Southern California, for instance. Your more immediate surroundings may suggest a different theme; for example, a large, woodsy lot might evoke a woodland garden, or a rural property might suggest a rustic garden. Or, your personal preferences may dictate the motif; perhaps you want to extend the eclectic style evident in your home furnishings to the outdoors.

If your space is small, choose a single garden style. Too many styles may overwhelm a small property or make the overall effect confusing or disjointed. In a large landscape, several distinct styles can coexist if they're separated visually—for example, by steps, walls, or tall shrubs.

Many styles may be interpreted either formally or informally, depending on your taste. Strictly formal gardens are known for their symmetry, straight or geometric lines, and plants clipped or trained into unnatural forms, as with sheared hedges or topiary. Informal gardens are characterized by a lack of symmetry and by flowing lines, curves, and natural-looking plant forms. Most slopes may be treated either formally or informally, though a formal approach to a steep incline can be quite expensive since it usually requires a lot of grading and terracing.

Of course, some styles wouldn't look right designed formally. A rustic or country garden should be informal; the same is true of a cottage garden, which should at least *look* unplanned and untamed. If you have a formal-looking house in an infor-

The mortared brick steps accented by neatly trimmed creeping fig at top are distinctly formal. The irregular stone-slab steps punctuated by sedum at bottom present a more casual appearance.

mal setting, you may want to use a few formal touches in the deck or patio to create a transition to the informal landscape.

Whatever general style you choose, try to put your own stamp on it. Your personal expression may be a piece of statuary that means something special to you, or it could take the form of whimsy—for example, planting in a found object, such as an old claw-foot bathtub. Another option is a collection of plants that you fancy, such as lavenders or roses.

REFINING YOUR LIST

Think again about the features you've listed to satisfy your landscaping objectives. Are they compatible with the garden style you favor? Do the "ABC's of Garden Design" (see page 84) make you think of elements you forgot—or do they make you realize that some features you've listed are superfluous?

Make any changes that you think will contribute to a better landscape. If the list of features is very long, whittle it down to the ones you like best. On the other hand, if the list is sketchy, try to fill in the blanks, including specifics about paving and other materials. While the goal is to refine your list, don't look at it as final; you will probably want to make changes as you develop your plan.

WHO'S IN CHARGE?

That's easy—you are in charge whether you plan the landscape on your own or not. It's your space and you should be satisfied with the result. In deciding whether to design the garden on your own or hire a professional, the most important question to ask is this: Do you really *want* to do it yourself? Unless budget is the sole consideration, it won't be worth the effort if it isn't any fun.

Next, consider the scale and complexity of the project and the extent of your landscaping expertise. If you're faced with creating an all-new landscape on a completely blank site; if your site presents complications such as chronic drainage problems, steep slopes, or an unusual lot shape; or if major construction is required, you may want a professional to handle the whole landscape or a part of it, such as a deck or a waterfall. But redesigning an existing small garden or adding a few simple elements is probably something you can complete on your own.

If you do consult a professional, that folder of garden ideas you've been compiling will be invaluable. It will communicate your preferences and desires better than words could.

This landscape combines elements of formality and informality. Pairs of planted ornamental pots—including two at the rear containing topiary—provide the main formal touches, while billowing screens of climbing roses contribute to an informal look.
Design: Jonathan Baille

Consider which materials to feature in your landscape. In this garden, cast concrete is the preferred medium: stepping-stones, boulders, the pond shell, and other features were sculpted to resemble natural stone. You might favor genuine stone, railroad ties, or used bricks—or perhaps a combination of materials.
Design: Harland Hand

ABC'S OF GARDEN DESIGN

Here are some concepts to keep in mind as you formulate your garden plan.

ACCENT

A gazebo, an ornamental sundial, a handsome specimen plant—each is a garden accent that attracts and holds the eye. On a very steep hillside, the right kind of accent can draw attention so that you notice more than just the slope. Don't overdo garden accents: an abundance of them is confusing to the eye.

ACCESS

You could view a hillside landscape solely from a patio or deck, but the garden will be much more versatile if you provide a way to get around and enjoy features meant for close-up viewing. Maintenance will also be easier; remember to leave room for garden carts or other equipment.

BALANCE

Try to distribute the total visual weight throughout the landscape—for example, don't confine color to a corner of the garden or along a wall. The garden design doesn't have to be symmetrical to be balanced.

COLOR

Work with a palette that pleases you. Don't stop with flower color; also include plants with colorful fruit, foliage, or bark. Consider the color of hardscape—for instance, gray gravel may be more agreeable than tan, and dull red bricks more attractive than red-orange ones.

FORM

Distinctive plant forms such as spiky or columnar shapes make good accents. Another option is to choose a form, such as an arch or a rectangle, and repeat it throughout the landscape—for example, in the shape of a gate, an arbor, an ornamental pool, and planting beds.

FRAGRANCE

Locate sweet-scented plants where you can enjoy the fragrance every day—for instance, near an entryway or a patio or deck. Placed beside a path, these plants will give you a reason to stop along the way.

LIGHTING

An inviting feature in any landscape, lighting is especially important on slopes for illuminating paths and stairways at night. Garden lighting should never shout; consider special effects such as soft uplights into trees.

PRIVACY

Structures such as fences and trellises offer immediate privacy but may be stark on their own. Plants have a softer appearance but may take years to reach screening size. Try a union of the two: vines trained on a trellis or shrubs grown against a fence. Before locating a privacy screen, check the sight lines to determine the screen's ideal height.

SIMPLICITY

Eliminate any extraneous details that don't contribute to your composition. Try repeating some elements instead of

introducing new ones, especially in very small gardens, but don't go overboard—the garden shouldn't be so simple that it's monotonous.

STRUCTURE

Every landscape needs permanent elements—trees and shrubs, statuary, seating, and paving, for example—to form a garden's bones. Use transitory features such as blooming annuals, perennials, and bulbs—many of which disappear or provide little interest for many months—to flesh out your framework.

UNITY

This intangible quality joins all parts of a garden into a pleasing whole. One way to achieve unity is to stick with a garden style. Another is through repetition: use the same brick or stonework throughout, the same plants in different places, the same color (gray and white are especially effective), or the same forms (see "Form"). Rather than design the landscape piecemeal, do it all at once even if you implement it in stages.

VARIETY

The trick is to add variety without mixing too many styles or making your space seem cluttered or chaotic. Think of quality rather than quantity; look for elements that create interest in the garden without complicating it. For example, include potted plants that can be replanted periodically, variegated-leaf plants, and plants with unusual textures or branching habits.

MAKING PLANS

Planning on paper isn't absolutely required, but it's a great way to get organized. Start with a base plan, an initial diagram showing all the features of your property. Next, doodle trial designs on tissue overlays. When you decide on a design, develop the final plan that will serve as a guide for installing the landscape. If you're landscaping only part of the yard, you may limit your drawings to that section but be sure to consider it in relation to the rest of the property.

As you plan, field-test your ideas to get a better sense of how they will work on a slope. The stepless path you've included may look good on paper, but it may feel too steep when you walk the route; the outline of a stream may seem just right on your plan, but when you lay it out in the backyard with ropes or stakes, you may decide that the curves need to be more exaggerated.

PRODUCING A BASE PLAN

A base plan, also called a site plan, is a scale drawing of the property and all permanent features. As its name implies, it is used as a base for further development of your landscape design. Slipping this plan under a sheet of tracing paper, you can easily experiment with designs.

This stage of planning involves a lot of measuring. You'll have a head start if you can find a parcel map or other survey of your property that contains boundary dimensions. Make sure that it reflects the current state of your lot and that there haven't been adjustments to the property lines since the map was produced. Dimensions on survey maps usually indicate distances measured on the level—that is, on a horizontal plane. You will be landscaping along the sloping distance, which is longer; however, the difference is usually significant only on very steep slopes.

If no map is available or you want to check distances along sloping terrain, take your own measurements. If you're unsure of the precise location of property lines, look for boundary markers. These are metal stakes that the original surveyor mapping your land drove into the ground at the corners of the plot; often the stakes are underground or hidden by brush. If there's any question about the boundaries, you may want to hire a surveyor to find the corners rather than risk building or planting on your neighbor's land.

Measure the site with a 50- or 100-foot tape. On a large property, you may pace off long distances; for example, you may discover that each of your strides equals 2 feet. Measuring is easier—especially on typically odd-shaped hillside lots—if you start with the house, then locate the property lines and other features (see the illustration at right).

As you measure—with a tape or by pacing—make rough diagrams, recording all dimensions and making notes. Indicate which direction is north. Note all slopes (with arrows showing their downhill direction) and low points. You may want to mark elevational differences at key spots; see page 13 for information on

BASE PLAN

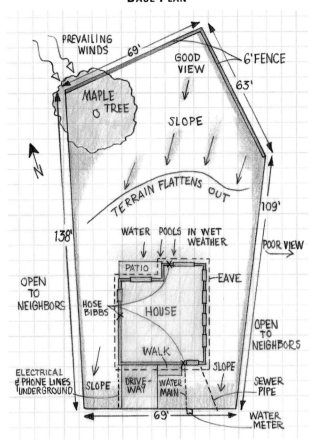

In this example of an odd-shaped lot, a moderate to steep slope flattens out behind the house and resumes its downward slant in the front yard.

PLOTTING YOUR PROPERTY

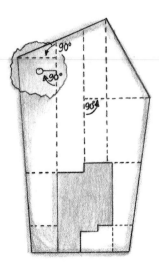

Here's an easy way to locate your house and other features within your property. First measure the house, then measure from each corner of the house to the adjoining property boundaries; line yourself up with the house wall to be sure you are proceeding in a straight line as you measure. To locate any property corners that don't line up with the house corners, angle off at a 90-degree angle from another line you've already measured or measure from an intermediate point along the house wall to the property corner. When you transfer the measurements to your site plan, connect the points along the boundaries to form the outline of your property. To locate a feature such as a tree or an outbuilding, measure straight from a known point, such as a house corner, and angle off at a 90-degree angle to the object.

In a base plan of this property, you would note that the hill slopes to a dip and then rises. Water collects in the gully in winter, making it too wet for most plants but a good location for a dry creekbed.

taking these measurements. Indicate all features that will influence your plan: structures, means of access, existing plants you want to save, sunny and shady areas, wind directions, aboveground and belowground utilities, and desirable as well as ugly views. Note all eaves, overhangs, downspouts, hose bibbs, drains, and irrigation lines. Locate the windows and doors on your house, and indicate the height of windowsills above the exterior grade.

Make a rough sketch of your property, incorporating all the features you've noted. Redraw the diagram to scale on graph paper or reproduce it on plain paper with the aid of an architect's scale—a triangular rule sold in many art supply and office supply stores. A scale of ¼ or ½ inch for 1 foot is typical for small spaces and ⅛ inch for 1 foot for larger ones.

ORGANIZING YOUR SPACE

To experiment with various arrangements of space, try the designer's trick of using "bubble diagrams." Draw bubbles—actually rough circles or ovals—to indicate the various elements or activity areas you've chosen to satisfy your landscaping goals. Each bubble should be roughly scaled to the size and shape needed (see the illustration below).

You can't just place features and activity areas randomly and expect a harmonious result. Look at the entire garden and lay out spaces that flow logically and easily from one to the other. Be sure to take into account the microclimates, potential views, and existing features identified on your site plan. Think about how the elements will be viewed from the house and from different spots within the garden. Also consider your slope when figuring out what to put where. Will a path suffice in this spot, or will you need some steps? Do you want to grade that uneven terrain for the gazebo, or should you locate it elsewhere? If you decide on grading to accommodate an element, don't grade within the drip line of an established tree unless you're prepared to spend a lot of money to protect the tree.

Plan a circulation path that won't require walking through a work area or past any unconcealed trash cans. Show any steps or stairways as sets of parallel lines.

Sketch as many versions as you like, then lay them out and compare the different arrangements of spaces. Settle on the one that will form the basis for your final design.

BUBBLE DIAGRAM

The bubbles represent elements that fulfill landscaping goals. Let's say that your goals are as follows: create privacy, deflect the force of the wind, take advantage of the pleasing view from the top of the hill, expand the seating area, grow flowers, keep water from puddling at the back of the house, hide trash cans, and make the front yard more appealing to passersby. In this example, the chosen solutions are tall shrubs along the boundaries to screen the property from neighbors and provide protection from winter winds, a gazebo where people can sit and enjoy the view, a large patio, flower beds, a dry creekbed to intercept water flowing downhill during wet weather, a vine-covered lath structure to screen trash cans and recycling bins at the side of the house, and terraced planting areas and a new front walkway traversing the front slope.

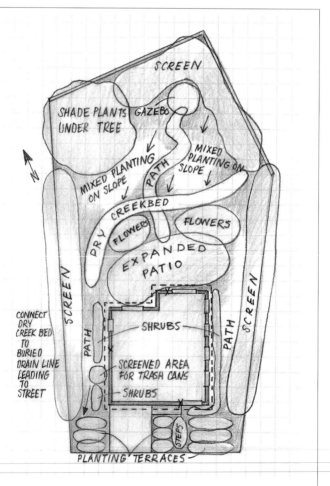

DEVELOPING THE FINAL PLAN

Once you've decided where everything goes, draw a plan showing the actual elements to scale. This "final" plan may require several revisions to get it the way you want.

First, indicate paths, seating areas, and other structures. Allow at least 2 feet of clearance between a path and a fence or other structure that is more than a couple of feet tall, so you won't swing your arms into it. Once structures are in place, concentrate on plants. You don't have to be specific right now; you may simply indicate "tall shrubs," "flower beds," and so on. Add provisions for other elements you may need, such as drainage. If you're unsure how much space to allot to a feature, try outlining it on the ground. If the size or shape doesn't look right, try again until the outline is a satisfactory one that you can transfer to your drawing.

After the main elements are pretty much in place, start selecting plants. (See page 123 for some plants useful in hillside gardens.) Consider growth habit, climate, and overall suitability to the style you're developing. Also consider the color each plant contributes. When locating plants, it's a good idea to group them according to their irrigation needs, especially in dry-summer regions. On the plan, draw a circle to represent each plant, roughly scaling it to the plant's width. (Garden references usually express width as a range; use the lower figure, especially in the cases of trees and shrubs, since the higher one may not apply for many years.)

Once everything is in place, redraw the plan neatly to scale. It will serve as your guide to installing the landscape—though you should allow yourself freedom to rearrange the plants in the garden if you think they look better another way. Make extra copies of the plan so that you can take one out into the garden and refer to it as you work.

FINAL PLAN labels: MAPLE TREE · GAZEBO · TALL SHRUBS · MIXED SHRUBS + GROUND COVERS · SHADE PLANTS · PATH · BRIDGE · DRY CREEK-BED · FLOWER BED · FLOWER BED · TALL SHRUBS · PATIO · PATH · LOW SHRUBS · HOUSE · LOW SHRUBS · SCREENED AREA FOR TRASH CANS · PATH · PLANTING TERRACES · DRIVEWAY · PLANTING TERRACES · STEPS

This is a version of a final plan with all structures and plantings in place but the plants still indicated in general terms. The next steps are to compile a list of plants and key them to the plan, indicating the quantity of each species or variety needed, and to redraw the plan.

PLANNING FOR DRAINAGE

Excess water coursing downhill may cause serious problems, including undermining foundations, flooding low-lying areas, and eroding hillsides. Before putting in a drainage system, you must figure out where the water is coming from, where you want to intercept it, and where to dispose of it. Be sure to get professional help with planning and installing a drainage system on a problem hillside.

Surface drains channel runoff along the ground. One type of surface drain is a

A patio like this one that's situated between a hillside and the house requires a drainage system to redirect water flowing down the slope. The patio surface is sloped toward a central drain (note the drain's grate). A drainpipe is also located behind the base of the retaining wall.

flume—an artificial channel or trough running down a slope. A dry creekbed designed as an ornamental feature can also serve as a surface drain during wet weather. Flexible plastic drainpipe that you attach to a downspout and direct away from the house is yet another kind of surface drain.

Subsurface drains carry away water underground. You may extend the flexible drainpipe attached to your downspout and run it a foot or so below ground to turn it into a subsurface drain. Another

During wet weather, subsurface water carried by drainpipe from the upper part of the landscape empties into a rock-filled channel.

subsurface device is a catch basin (see opposite page) with a solid-surface drainpipe to carry the water to a more suitable disposal area. Drainpipes are also available that are perforated to allow some water to seep into the soil while the excess is routed away. A French drain that incorporates perforated pipe in a gravel-filled trench is one of the most common types of subsurface drains (see below). You can also increase the effectiveness of a dry creekbed as a drainage channel by laying perforated drainpipe in the bottom (see page 119).

In most cities and suburbs, drainage devices divert excess water to the street and storm sewers. In outlying or rural areas, you may be able to direct moisture to a ravine. Another type of drain is a dry well—a gravel-filled hole about 3 feet wide and at least as deep that allows water to soak into the soil. It's best suited to locations with fast-draining soil and flat or slightly sloping terrain; on steeper grades, water tends to accumulate too quickly in the well.

FRENCH DRAIN

This drainage device is a gravel-filled trench with perforated pipe in the bottom, though some say that a true French drain contains just gravel and no pipe. Water percolates through the gravel into the soil; if a drainpipe is included, it routes any excess water to a disposal area.

The trench is typically 2 to 4 feet deep and at least a foot wide. If you're trying to protect a structure such as a garage floor, the trench should be deep enough so that the pipe sits below the floor level. If the French drain is to be on flat ground, slope the drainpipe to keep water moving. (Slant it about 2 percent toward the uncapped end—that translates to a drop of 2 feet for every 100 feet or about 2½ inches for every 10 feet.) If you're locating the drain on a slope, just run it parallel to the ground. The open end of the pipe should be directed toward a disposal site. You may want to connect the perforated drainpipe to a solid-surface drainpipe that carries the water to the disposal point.

To install a French drain, dig the trench and line it with landscape fabric, making sure there's enough overlap on either side so that you can wrap the fabric around the drainpipe and several inches of drain rock or gravel. Lay the pipe at the bottom of the trench, with the perforations facing downward. Install a cleanout at the high point of the pipe. Backfill

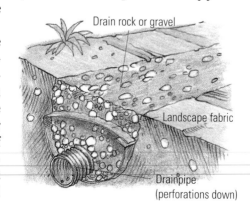

Drain rock or gravel

Landscape fabric

Drainpipe
(perforations down)

When it rains, this dry creekbed with a drainpipe buried at the bottom intercepts water flowing down the slope.

Design: Johnsen Landscapes and Pools

the trench with about 4 inches of drain rock or gravel (be sure the pieces are bigger than the holes in the pipe) and wrap the landscape fabric all the way around it. Fill the trench to the top with additional gravel or rock. If you want to plant on top of the trench, fill it to the top with compacted soil instead and avoid using plants with deep or invasive roots.

CATCH BASIN

To drain water from a low-lying area, dig a hole for a catch basin at the lowest point. Then, leading from the side opening in the basin, dig a trench for a solid-surface drainpipe that will carry the water to a disposal site, such as a storm drain. Either set a ready-made

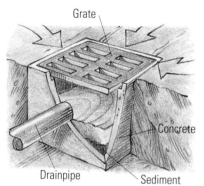

Grate

Drainpipe

Concrete

Sediment

catch basin (sold at building supply stores) into the hole, or form and pour a concrete basin yourself. Fill in soil around the sides of the basin, and set a grate on top. The bottom of the basin serves as a sediment trap, catching debris and dirt so that they don't enter the drainpipe.

CONTROLLING SOIL EROSION

Hillside properties are especially prone to soil erosion because water running downhill carries soil away with it. A drainage system that intercepts runoff and reroutes it to a disposal area is one way to protect the slope.

Slowing the runoff by placing obstacles in its path is another effective curb because it gives the water more time to soak into the ground. You can use open or framed terraces, retaining walls,

Riprap (below left) and simple terraces made from landscape timbers (below right) are two effective ways to reduce the speed of runoff and help protect the slope from wearing away.

Obstacles such as landscape timbers may be set into a hillside to slow and divert the downward flow of water. Use as many timbers as you need for control.

riprap (a loose arrangement of stones), and baffles such as railroad ties, landscape timbers, or logs. Both the stones used in the riprap slopes and the baffles are partially buried in the hillside.

Among the best erosion controls are plants whose roots thoroughly permeate the soil and whose foliage breaks the force of falling water; see page 123 for some suitable plants. Be sure to mulch any bare soil around the plants.

The way a landscape is installed can help preserve a slope or wear it away even faster. If you plan to install the garden over several years, restrict any grading or clearing to areas that you're dealing with now. Because well-rooted plants hold the soil, preserve as much of the existing vegetation as possible. Plant as soon as possible after grading. In areas that get heavy winter rains, plan any construction for spring and summer so that the erosion-control measures are in place before the rainy season. If for some reason you're unable to plant before rains begin, cover the soil with black plastic, making sure it's in close contact with the soil and well anchored. As an alternative, sow grass as a temporary planting to stabilize the soil.

Some constructed features are perfect additions to hillsides. They may be necessary elements, like steps and retaining walls on a steep slope, or nonessential but "gotta have"

BUILDING ON
SLOPES

features, such as decks and water-falls that highlight a site's sloping ter-rain. Other items, like fences, are simply more challenging to build on slopes than on level ground. With still others, such as paths and patios, the goal is to find suitable flattish or easily leveled land on which to construct them.

This chapter explains what factors you need to consider when building various landscape features on a slope. Emphasis is placed on projects that the average do-it-yourselfer might tackle rather than on ones requiring more expertise, such as poured concrete patios or walls. Be realistic about which activities you can undertake yourself and which require the help of a contractor or other landscaping professional.

Safety is always important, but especially so when you're working on a slope. When moving heavy materials, enlist helpers; don't take a chance on a large rock or a gravel-filled wheelbarrow getting away from you.

Constructed elements on this moderate slope include flagstone steps and a meandering watercourse with a series of waterfalls and small pools.

Design: Robert Howard

STEPS AND STAIRWAYS

When slopes have a grade of at least 10 percent (a rise or fall of 1 foot for every 10 feet of distance), steps are essential for easy navigation. On gentler grades, steps aren't usually necessary, although you may want some for surer footing or design purposes. Choose a material that complements the garden's style but doesn't compromise safety; the steps should not pose a hazard in wet weather.

RISER-TREAD RELATIONSHIP

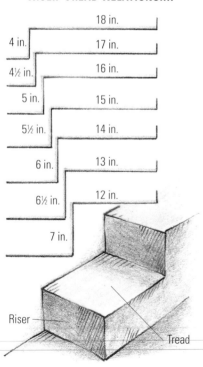

Riser

Tread

FIGURING STEP PROPORTIONS

Well-designed steps have good proportions: the height of the risers (the vertical part of the steps) relative to the depth of the treads (the horizontal part) allows for comfortable climbing. The shorter the riser, the deeper the tread should be; conversely, the taller the riser, the shorter the tread should be. A handy formula for figuring a good riser-tread ratio is to make sure twice the riser height plus the depth of the tread in inches equals 26 (see the chart below left for some examples). Some landscape designers incorporate wiggle room into the equation by expressing the total as a range: 25 to 27.

For maximum comfort in climbing outdoor steps, make the riser no lower than 4 inches and no higher than 7 inches—the middle range (5 to 6 inches) is considered ideal. For safety's sake, make all the steps in any one stairway uniform in size.

FITTING STEPS TO A SLOPE

To construct a stairway between two fixed points, you must first gauge the change in level between those points. This requires measuring the height of the slope (A to B in the drawing), as well as the horizontal distance, or run (A to C). To calculate the number of steps you will need, divide the desired riser height into the slope height (in inches); drop any fractional remainder. Divide the whole number into the slope height to determine the exact height for each riser. Now find the corresponding tread size on the riser-tread ratio chart. To determine whether the steps will fit into

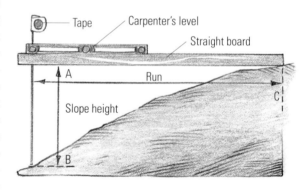

the run, multiply the tread size by the number of steps. For a proper fit, the resulting number should be approximately equal to the run from A to C.

Rarely will steps of the proportions you've chosen fit a slope exactly as it is. You may be able to force a fit by making minor adjustments in the riser and tread dimensions, or you may have to cut and fill the slope to accommodate the steps. If the slope is too steep for even 7-inch risers, remember that a stairway need not run straight up and down. One solution is to take the stairs through curves or switchbacks; another is to break up the flight of steps with one or more landings.

TIE OR TIMBER STEPS

Railroad ties or pressure-treated landscape timbers make simple, rugged risers that may be teamed with your choice of tread material. Many railroad ties are 8 feet long and can be conveniently cut in half for 4-foot-wide steps, although their widths—which become the steps' riser height—may vary somewhat. Landscape timbers come in a range of lengths and more uniform widths.

Installation is fairly easy. Excavate the site to accommodate the shape of the steps, firmly tamping the soil. After cutting the wood to the proper length, drill a 1-inch hole near each end. Lay the risers in place on the stairway so they don't rock or wobble, then use a sledgehammer to drive 18-inch-long, 1/2-inch galvanized steel pipes or 3/4-inch reinforcing bars through the holes into the ground. Hammer the rods flush with the tops of the lumber.

If the soil is not firm, you may want stronger support for the risers. Instead of securing them to the ground, pour small concrete footings and set anchor bolts in the slightly hardened concrete. When the concrete has set (after about 2 days), secure predrilled and counterbored ties or timbers to the bolts with nuts and washers.

Once the risers are in place, excavate the tread spaces behind them to receive gravel, bricks, stones, concrete pieces, mulch, or other material. Compact the soil well before filling in the treads. Flat stones, broken pieces of concrete, and mulch don't need edging to keep them in place. The simplest way to place stone or concrete treads is directly in soil; mulch treads are even easier—just spread the material.

Both gravel and brick treads do require containment; edgings of 2-inch-wide lumber or fieldstones are attractive choices. For gravel treads (see below), you may lay a 1-inch base of sand and compact it before adding the gravel—or just place the gravel on the excavated soil. For brick-on-sand treads, be sure to dig deep enough to accommodate the bricks plus a 2-inch bed of sand. Set the bricks on the compacted sand, tap them into place, and level them. Brush sand into the joints, and apply a fine spray from a garden hose to settle the sand.

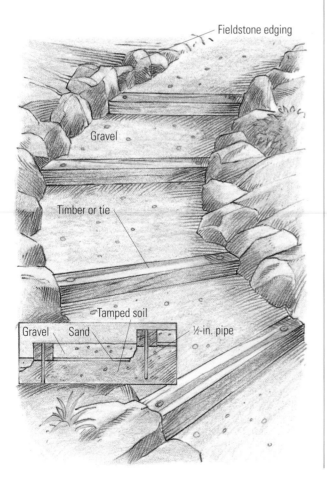

Fieldstone edging

Gravel

Timber or tie

Tamped soil

Gravel   Sand   ½-in. pipe

PLANNING POINTERS

As you design garden steps, be sure to keep the following guidelines in mind.

- Make the steps at least as wide as the path. They may be much broader if you want to incorporate seating, planters, or other elements.

- The closer that steps come to allowing a normal walking stride, the safer and easier they are to climb. If you make steps too low (shorter than 4 inches), you will find yourself taking them two at a time, which can be dangerous, particularly if you're carrying something with both hands.

- For drainage, slope the surface of each tread 1 to 2 percent (⅛ to ¼ inch per foot) toward its riser. As an alternative, slope the treads sideways to run water into a channel at the edge of the steps.

- Avoid using just one step along a pathway because people won't expect it and may trip over it. Either fit in a second step or eliminate steps altogether and zigzag or curve a sloping path up the hillside instead.

- On gentle to moderate slopes, you may opt for "ramp steps" (see below). Make the ramp length uniform—for example, 6, 8, or 10 feet—so that people walking along it can anticipate the next step. The ramp's slope can approach 10 percent and still be comfortable to navigate.

- If the steps traverse a steep slope, include landings—each a minimum of 4 feet long—to break up the staircase visually and make it less daunting to climb. At each landing, consider including something interesting to view, such as a feature plant or pottery.

On gentle to moderate slopes, a succession of single steps with long ramps between them may take the place of a standard stairway. Because the steps are repeated, they don't pose the tripping hazard that a lone step does.

Design: Conni Cross

STONE LOOK-ALIKE

This stairway is made from cast concrete that was sculpted to resemble natural stone. Low-growing plants between the steps add charm and soften the appearance of the hard surface.

Design: Harland Hand

STEPPING-STONE STAIRWAY

This is a relatively easy way to take a path up a slope. It works especially well for casual steps in private parts of the landscape where foot traffic isn't high. For secure footing, choose thick, flat, sturdy stones at least 20 inches long and 2 feet wide.

Starting at the downhill end of the slope, excavate a hole that is deep enough to accommodate a 2-inch sand base and a partially buried stone. Wet the sand and tamp it well. (If your soil is unstable or if it drains poorly, then dig a deeper hole and install 4 to 6 inches of tamped gravel before adding the sand.) Lay the stone in the hole and twist it into the sand until it is level and firmly embedded.

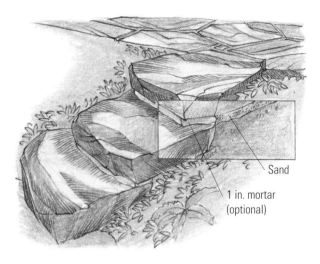

Sand

1 in. mortar (optional)

After setting the first stone, position the next stone overlapping the first one a few inches for stability. You can spread a 1-inch layer of mortar on the back of the lower step to bond the stones where they touch, although both stones must be very securely set for the bond to hold. Mortar may be more useful in filling incompatible contours where the stones meet. Build additional steps as needed.

These stepping-stones ascend a steep slope. Instead of overlapping, the stones are spaced apart as for a path, with gaps of 4 to 6 inches between them, and very firmly embedded into the slope to support the weight of people scaling them. The riser height created by spacing the stones apart is greater than if the stones overlapped, making for a more comfortable climb. Also, fewer stones are needed, reducing the cost of the stairway.

Design: Betty Edwards

Unless the stones are very thick, the risers will be lower than recommended for comfortable climbing, but that shouldn't pose a problem for an informal path away from main walkways, especially if the treads are deep. For a stepping-stone stairway in which the stones don't overlap, see the bottom photograph on the opposite page.

You can also build a stairway with concrete stepping-stones cast in place. The construction method is the same as for making a concrete stepping-stone path (see page 98). Overlap the steps by casting the upper steps partially onto the lower ones.

MASONRY STEPS

Steps may consist solely of poured concrete, or the concrete may be used as a base for mortared masonry units, such as bricks, flagstones, or tiles. Unless you have experience building forms and pouring concrete, you may want to leave this project to a professional. Here is the basic procedure for building this type of stairway.

First, excavate rough steps in the soil. Allow space for at least a 6-inch gravel setting bed and a 4-inch thickness of concrete on both treads and risers. (In cold climates you will need 6 to 8 inches of concrete, plus a footing that is sunk below the frost line.) Account for the thickness of any masonry units in step dimensions. Compact the soil well.

From 2-inch-thick lumber, build forms to hold the concrete. Lay the gravel, keeping it 4 inches back from the front of the steps; this way, the concrete will be extra thick at those potentially weak points. Set 6-inch-square welded wire mesh on spacers to reinforce the concrete.

Pour the concrete and level it with the tops of the forms. To make concrete treads more weather safe, broom the wet concrete to roughen its surface. (Don't broom the surface if you plan on mortaring other materials on top.) To cure the concrete, cover it with a plastic sheet for 2 days, then remove the forms. Mortar any bricks or other masonry units onto the cured concrete.

A BENEFICIAL MERGER

Two indispensable components of hillside landscaping—steps and retaining walls—are often combined. Both benefit aesthetically: the steps break up the wall's expanse, and the wall adds interest to the stairway. The construction materials needn't be the same, but in this case natural stone unifies the two elements.

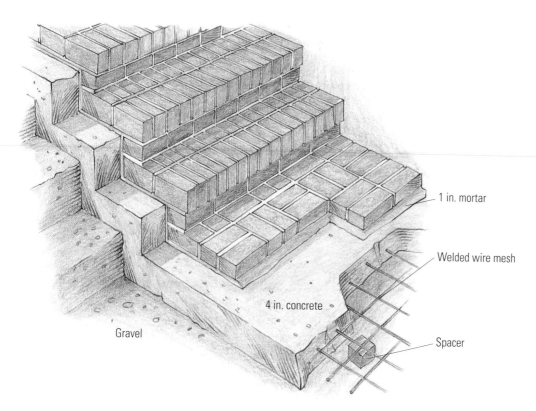

1 in. mortar

Welded wire mesh

4 in. concrete

Spacer

Gravel

Paths

Any landscape needs pathways for directing traffic and providing access to various parts of the garden. On sloping terrain, paths are usually linked with steps to form a circulation system. If you want to limit the number of steps — perhaps for cost reasons or so you can roll a garden cart more easily — keep that in mind when planning the path's route. Also, choose the path material carefully; some materials hold more securely on sloping ground.

REDUCING THE STEEPNESS OF THE CLIMB

You can plot a direct path up a slope (top), but curving it (bottom) makes the climb more gradual and may eliminate the need for steps.

PLOTTING A PATH

A direct route is quicker, but a meandering one is often more attractive, especially when interesting sights or experiences — accent plants, water features, resting spots — unfold along the way. A circuitous route is also more practical on hilly terrain: curving or zigzagging the path decreases the steepness of the climb. The ideal slope for walkways is between 1 and 5 percent (a little over 1 inch to 6 inches of rise or fall for every 10 feet of distance), although the grade can be as steep as 10 percent (1 foot for every 10 feet) before steps are necessary.

An entrance walkway should be at least 4 feet wide; 6 feet allows two people to walk abreast. For an informal garden path, 3 feet is the usual minimum width, although narrower paths are acceptable where space is limited. Be sure any path is wide enough to accommodate a wheelbarrow or other equipment that will be regularly conveyed along it.

Even if you do some preliminary planning on paper, there's no better way to decide on the course of a path than in the landscape, where you can experience for yourself how comfortable it is to ascend a certain grade or how a twist or bend in the route affects the climb. Garden hoses or lengths of rope are useful for marking the path, or staking flags or wooden stakes may be inserted along the proposed pathway; spray water-soluble paint along a staked perimeter to visualize the path more clearly. If you're not happy with the layout, you can easily alter it before you start constructing the path.

PATH MATERIALS

Many types of building materials may be used to make garden walkways. In a hillside garden, you may choose from the full range of materials — if you construct nearly level paths and put in steps to bridge them. Significantly sloping paths limit your choices. Gravity tugs on loose material such as gravel, and although mortared bricks or stone will stay in place, the walking surface may become hazardous in wet weather or in icy conditions.

GRAVEL

A gravel path is among the simplest, most economical to construct. The path may traverse a slope, but the grade must be modest or the material will slide downhill. Even on slight inclines, you'll have to add more gravel periodically to maintain the path. To keep the gravel from spreading sideways into the garden, use an edging.

Gravel may be formed naturally or manufactured by mechanically crushing large pieces of stone. In either case, the pieces are usually graded to a uniform size. A ⅝-inch gravel is comfortable underfoot. Pieces larger than ¾ inch may be too bumpy, and a very fine gravel may be too dusty. Various colors, primarily browns and grays, are available.

Natural gravel has rounded edges, which are hard to compress into a firm walking surface and are best used for decorative purposes. Pea gravel falls into this category — it rolls and scatters when walked on. Crushed rock is preferable for paths because the sharp-edged or angular pieces compact tightly, making a more stable base.

Decomposed granite (d.g.), which is often sold as a form of gravel, consists of naturally degraded stone particles ranging in size from small gravel to sand. Some people use it as a base for a pathway, and others as the top surface. It compresses extremely well and is long lasting. Road base is another excellent, easily compacted base for gravel.

MULCH

Organic mulch is ideal for creating informal, natural-looking paths through the garden, but don't use it on main walks leading to the house, as you'll track it indoors. Not only is a mulched path inexpensive, but it's also extremely simple to install. Just spread

1

LAYING A GRAVEL PATH

3

1 Install the edging first; in this example, fieldstones form the path boundaries. Put down landscape fabric, if you like, to deter weeds, and pour a base of sand or crushed rock over the site.

2 Rake the sand or crushed rock to a uniform 1-inch thickness. As you rake, wet the material with a fine spray.

3 Tamp the wet base several times, packing it down firmly.

4 Spread gravel at least 2 inches thick and rake it evenly over the base. Tamp the gravel firmly into place.

2

4

the mulch on the soil surface—there's no need to trench or install edgings.

Shredded tree trimmings (sometimes sold as arbor mulch) are especially good because they contain materials of various sizes that fit together and compact on a gentle slope. Check whether your municipality offers recycled prunings free or at low cost to local residents, or look around your own property for other material you could use as mulch, such as fallen pine needles.

BRICK

Choose brick that will provide traction and stand up in cold climates (see page 113). A brick path may be set on a base of sand or mortar. Setting the bricks in sand is easier and less expensive, but the path must be fairly level and securely edged to keep the sand in place and the bricks from dislodging. Add the sand base and compact it. Set the bricks on the sand and level them; sweep sand between the cracks, then settle the sand with a fine spray from a garden hose.

The bricks will be more stable if mortared to a concrete pad. As with any poured concrete work, building the pad is usually a job for a professional.

STEPPING-STONES

Pavers of various sizes and shapes are sold as stepping-stones, but not all are substantial enough to stay put, especially through frosts and heavy rains. Choose a thick, heavy material, such as flagstone, broken concrete, or cast concrete. These materials may be set directly in soil, can follow gently rolling terrain, and are easily combined with steps made of the same or a complementary material.

Lay out the stepping-stones the way you think you want them and check the arrangement for aesthetics and walking comfort. For concrete stepping-stones that will be cast in place, tear newspaper into irregular shapes and arrange the pieces on the ground. Large gaps between stepping-stones encourage people to hurry along; small gaps slow people down. On a functional path, gaps of 10 to 12 inches work well, but for a leisurely tour through an ornamental part of the garden, make the gaps 4 to 6 inches. Keep in mind that large stones look best separated by large spaces; large stones with a smooth surface will also provide sure footing. When building a path for a slower pace, you may use smaller stepping-stones (but don't choose any less than 18 inches long), and the surface may be rougher.

STONES. You can get natural stones with irregular edges or stones cut into geometric shapes. Choices of color and texture

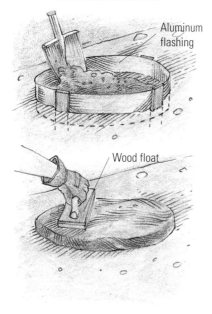

Aluminum
flashing

Wood float

Dig a hole in the ground; if desired, use aluminum flashing or other flexible material to extend the form above grade. Shovel in wet concrete, then tamp it and use a wood float to smooth the surface.

tend to vary by region. Flagstones sold for paving are usually between 1 and 2 inches thick. For the most stable surface, select large pieces of thick stone.

CONCRETE. You can buy big, sturdy precast concrete stepping-stones; use large chunks of broken concrete with the rough side down; or cast stepping-stones of any size or shape you want in molds dug in the ground. Irregular blocks that vary in size have the uneven look of natural stepping-stones, whereas large rectangles or other geometric shapes are more formal-looking.

When casting a stone in the ground, dig a hole 4 inches deep and fill it with ready-mix concrete. For irregular blocks that rise above the ground, try using a flexible material like aluminum flashing as a form for each stone; bend it into the desired shape and stake it on the outside. Fill the mold, tamp the wet concrete, and smooth the surface with a wood float. To make it look more like a real stone, try sculpting it: give it a somewhat uneven surface and leave little depressions where moss can grow. You can also add color by mixing a tint with mortar and using it as a top layer. Keep the stepping-stones damp for several days to cure the concrete.

POURED CONCRETE

This material makes a stable walking surface on gently sloping terrain, especially if it is textured or pattern-stamped to provide traction in wet weather. It can also be tinted to add interest and soften the look of the walkway. A poured concrete path may be complicated and/or costly, depending on what you can do yourself and the size and finish of the walkway. Unless you've had experience in construction, you'll want to call in a qualified professional to construct the forms, pour the concrete, and finish the surface.

PATH EDGINGS

Edgings are essential to keep some path materials from migrating or dislodging. Install them after the soil has been graded but before the setting bed and paving are laid. String mason's line around the perimeter to mark the exact borders of the path as well as to designate the top of the edging. To achieve the correct edging height, dig narrow trenches under the lines.

LAYING STEPPING-STONES IN SOIL

1 Arrange the stepping-stones in a pleasing pattern on top of the soil. Place them so the spaces between them allow for a comfortable, regular pace.

2 Cut around each stone with a spade (or a knife) to mark its shape, and then move the stone to one side.

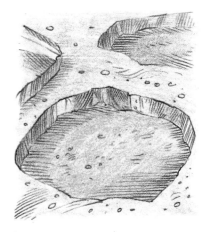

3 Excavate a hole for the stone using a straight-edged spade. So that the stone will rise above grade, make the hole half as deep as the stone's thickness, plus 1 inch deeper for the sand base.

A path routed across a hillside encounters fewer changes in elevation than one that runs up and down the slope. Even so, the path area usually must be graded, which often creates a ridge just above it. A very low retaining wall solves the problem of holding the soil on the uphill side. Here, a low stone wall not only holds the earth above a gravel path, but it also forms the path's uphill edging. Additional stones serve as the downhill edging.

A wood edging must be rot resistant: use either pressure-treated lumber or the heartwood of redwood, cedar, or cypress. For straight lines, use standard lumber (usually 2 by 4s or 2 by 6s) set on edge and staked every few feet. For curves, use a triple layer of flexible benderboard (standard size is ³⁄₈ inch thick by 4 inches wide). For information on working with benderboard, see at right.

A rustic or woodsy landscape is a good setting for an edging of fieldstones. When carefully laid, they can appear natural and achieve their task of containing the path. You don't need to dig a trench for the stones; just twist them into the soil so they sit firmly.

A brick-in-soil edging is tidy and easy to construct, but it needs very firm soil to hold the bricks in place. To install the bricks, mark off and dig a narrow trench. Set the bricks side by side, on end, in the trench; level them to get the tops even (you may bury the bricks so the tops are flush with the finished path). After you've set the edging, pack soil against the outside of the bricks, tamping firmly.

Other options include plastic and metal edging strips, which are flexible enough for use on curves. Secure the strips by driving stakes through a channel or slots, then conceal the outer edge of the strips with soil or mulch.

Poured concrete makes a neat, secure edging, but it requires more expertise to install than the other materials. It can be used as an invisible edging underground, a base for an edging of brick, or a decorative ribbon of concrete flush with the path.

INSTALLING BENDERBOARD

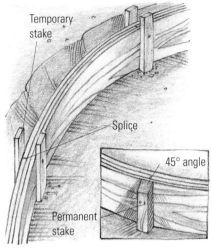

Dig a trench about 5 inches deep, and wide enough for three layers of benderboard. Set the three layers loosely together in the trench, staggering the ends so that splices in one layer are at least 2 feet away from splices in another; put temporary stakes on both sides of the edging at each splice. (For sharp curves, first soak the wood in water for about 30 minutes so it will bend more easily.)

When all the benderboard is laid out, replace each pair of temporary stakes with a single, permanent stake on the outside of the edging that is 2 by 2 by 18 inches (12 inches in very rocky or hard soil). Drive in the permanent stakes so they're about even with the top of the benderboard, then push the layers of wood together, squeeze out the air, and nail to the stakes. Saw off the tops of the stakes even with the top of the benderboard, sloping the cut back at a 45-degree angle so that the stakes will be invisible when the edging is finished. Backfill the trench with soil.

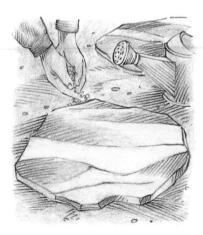

4 Spread 1 inch of sand in the hole, and wet it with a fine spray. Place the stone in the hole and twist it into the sand until the stone is level and firm.

5 Add more sand around and beneath the stone if necessary; water the sand to finish setting the stone.

RETAINING WALLS

These structures are different from freestanding garden walls because they must withstand the force of soil pushing against them. Depending on the steepness of the slope and the height of the wall, the pressure can be tremendous, especially when heavy rains and melting snow saturate the soil. That's why careful planning is important in the siting, design, and construction of a retaining wall.

PLANNING THE WALL

Simple, low retaining walls on gently sloping, stable ground are manageable do-it-yourself projects. You may want to install a single wall at the base of a slope, or terrace the slope with a series of walls. Most of the construction materials used for retaining walls are heavy; a helper will make the job go faster. For a tall wall or where extensive grading is required or the ground is unstable or steep, you'll need to call in a professional—usually a licensed engineer or landscape contractor.

Most retaining walls in home landscapes are made of wood, stone, or concrete. In choosing a wall material, take into account not just aesthetics and cost, but also the material's suitability for a particular job. For example, staked boards are fine for a low wall on a gentle slope but completely inadequate for a high wall on a steep hill. Consider, too, who will be building the wall. Construction professionals can handle any material, but do-it-yourselfers typically want something easy to work with, like modular concrete blocks, railroad ties, or boards.

Many municipalities require building permits for all retaining walls, while some don't have any requirements for structures up to a specified height (often 3 feet); check with your local building department. Also find out how close to the property line you may build and whether the wall you intend to construct needs a concrete footing or steel reinforcement. You may be required to place the foundation for certain types of walls a certain depth below ground, especially in areas where the ground freezes. Save yourself trouble later on by gathering all the necessary information before you begin building.

STABILITY AND DRAINAGE

You can build stability into a retaining wall in various ways. The most important way is to locate the wall

GRADING FOR A RETAINING WALL

It's best to site your retaining wall so that it causes the least possible disruption of the natural slope. In each of the situations shown here, the retaining wall rests on cut or undisturbed ground, not on fill. Whichever design you choose, plan to use excavated soil as fill behind the wall so that you won't have to import soil or have any soil hauled away.

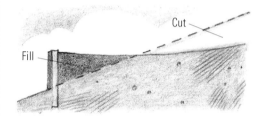

The slope is cut away and excess earth is moved downhill. The retaining wall now holds back a long terrace.

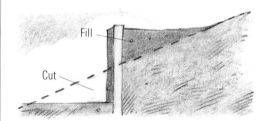

Soil is cut away and moved behind a tall retaining wall. The result is level ground below and a high terrace behind the wall.

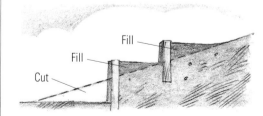

Total wall height is divided between two terraces, resulting in a series of level beds.

Tight joints between stones and a gradual tilt—or batter—of the wall back into the slope build stability into a dry-laid stone retaining wall.

on undisturbed or cut ground—never on fill, which is more prone to erosion and movement. If you're terracing a slope, start with the bottom retaining wall and work upward (doing it the other way around might undermine the wall you've just built).

Even if the wall you're building doesn't require a footing, set the first layer of wall materials below grade. When stacking stones or concrete modular blocks without mortar (called dry-stacking), lean the face of the wall back into the slope to increase stability; this lean is called the batter or cant (see at right). To keep soil from oozing through the open joints of a dry-stacked wall and gradually eroding the slope, you can place landscape fabric—a lightweight material used as a weed barrier—between the soil and the wall.

When a retaining wall fails, poor drainage is usually the cause. Solid walls—those with mortared joints or made of poured concrete—may burst if water is allowed to dam up behind the wall. Dry-stacked walls are self-draining to some degree because water can filter through joints in the wall, although added drainage makes them more stable. The most common type of drainage is a gravel backfill behind the wall. Water that collects in the gravel can be drained off in one of two ways: weep holes may be built into the base of the wall (although water flowing through these holes tends to stain the wall over time) or a drainpipe may be positioned behind the wall to channel the water to a storm sewer or other disposal area. To install a drainpipe, lay the perforated side down on the gravel at the base of the wall with the open end of the pipe extending toward the disposal area. Pack gravel under the capped end as needed so that the pipe slopes toward the open end about ¼ inch per foot.

Be sure that the soil behind the retaining wall is well compacted. Don't just shovel in earth and tamp down the top; add the fill in 6-inch layers and compact each layer thoroughly before adding more.

A Battered Wall

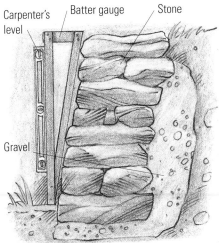

Battering, or slanting, a dry-stacked wall into the slope about 2 inches per foot of rise helps to stabilize it. To take the guesswork out of the tilt, make a batter gauge from strips of 1-by-2 wood. Nail together at right angles a vertical piece equal to the height of the wall and a horizontal piece equal to the batter at the top of the wall; for example, using the formula above, the batter for a 3-foot-tall wall would be 6 inches. Nail a third strip of wood to the ends of the other strips to form a triangle. To check the batter of the wall as you're building it, hold the vertical strip plumb against a level.

STRONG TIES

The corner joints of this railroad-tie retaining wall are staggered for added strength, and the side walls are tapered into the hillside.

A BOARD RETAINING WALL

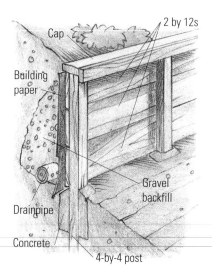

Cap
2 by 12s
Building paper
Gravel backfill
Drainpipe
Concrete
4-by-4 post

WOOD WALLS

These are best kept low, to about 3 feet tall, and built on a base of firm, compacted soil. To prolong the life of the wall, use wood that's rot resistant (redwood, cedar, or cypress) or pressure treated. Rough, unfinished wood is well suited to the job. Cap the wall with wide boards (usually 2 by 8s or 2 by 10s) to have it double as a bench.

TIES OR TIMBERS

Top-quality railroad ties make good material for retaining walls, but if your choices are limited to ties that ooze creosote or are crooked or studded with nails, you may opt for a substitute—landscape timbers. They don't have the weathered charm of genuine ties, but they are more uniform. Railroad-tie dimensions range from about 6 by 6 to 7 by 9 inches wide and 8 to 8½ feet long. Timbers come in a wider variety of sizes.

Ties or timbers are usually laid horizontally. To begin, partially bury the first course of wood. For added strength, set each additional course back about an inch and stagger the joints. Anchor the wall to the ground by pounding galvanized steel pipe or reinforcing bar into holes drilled through the ties or timbers; the holes should be spaced about 4 feet apart. Use long rods so that at least as much steel is in the ground as above it.

As an alternative, you may place the ties or timbers vertically. Stand them on end, with about two-thirds of their height underground. To strengthen the wall, set the ends in concrete and fasten a continuous strip of sheet metal, such as flashing, to the back with wide-headed nails.

TIES OR TIMBERS LAID HORIZONTALLY

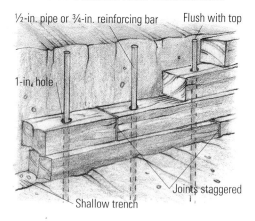

½-in. pipe or ¾-in. reinforcing bar
Flush with top
1-in. hole
Shallow trench
Joints staggered

TIES OR TIMBERS LAID VERTICALLY

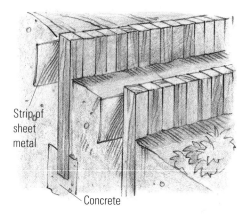

Strip of sheet metal
Concrete

BOARDS

For a board wall, use wide planks connected to 4-by-4 posts. Select posts twice the height of the finished wall, since half of each post will be buried. Position the posts no more than 4 feet apart; see page 116 for information on setting them. When attaching the boards, stagger the joints so they don't all line up at the same posts. For visible posts, nail or screw the boards to the posts on the upslope side of the wall. For hidden posts, attach the boards to the front of the posts with carriage bolts, which have attractive rounded heads. Use four bolts at each splice and two on boards that span a post. Line the back of the wall with moisture-proof building paper to extend the wall's life by several years.

DRY WALLS

Large, stackable units like stones and broken concrete pieces may be laid in courses without mortar; their weight holds them in place. Modular concrete-block wall systems developed with the do-it-yourselfer in mind and widely available at home improvement centers are meant to be laid dry.

Dry walls don't need concrete footings if they're kept fairly low (to about 3 feet tall). The foundation may be a 4- to 6-inch-thick pad of well-compacted angular gravel, crushed stone, road base, or coarse sand. Don't use pea gravel or other rounded gravel for the pad or backfill, because these materials don't compress well. Dig a 2-foot-wide trench deep enough to accommodate the pad and a partially buried first course; use a carpenter's level to check that the foundation is even. If the length of the wall is on sloping terrain, you may have to create a stepped foundation. Start building the wall at the lowest elevation.

STONE

Depending on the stones and how they're arranged, a dry-stone wall may be casual and unassuming or strictly formal in appearance. The stones may be cut or uncut. Homeowners with stony soil may find they don't have to purchase rocks—there may be enough on their land to construct one or more walls.

For a traditional dry-stone wall, stack the stones, placing larger ones on the bottom and stepping each course back slightly so that the face leans into the slope (see page 101). If you are using uncut stones, either cut or knock off pieces with a short-handled sledgehammer or a mason's hammer as needed to make tight joints. Stagger the joints so that a full stone sits above the juncture of two stones—"one stone over two, two over one," according to the stonemason's rule.

Riprap is a type of informal, natural-looking stone wall that is easy to build and doesn't need a leveling pad. It is a loose arrangement of stones with one or more layers placed directly against an existing slope or bank (see at top right). For stability, partially bury the bottom layer of stones.

MODULAR CONCRETE BLOCKS

This type of wall system uses precast concrete blocks that stack or lock together by means of lips, pins, or friction. The blocks are available in various shapes, colors, and textures. Some have a uniform, manufactured appearance, while others are more natural-looking. With modular wall systems, a batter is built in; among the different block styles, the setback ranges from subtle to stair step in appearance. All types allow you to turn corners and arrange the blocks in curves.

If you use blocks with a rear lip, consider how you will lay the first row. The blocks may be placed with the lip at the rear facing downward and embedded in the base, or they may be installed upside down and backward (as shown in the illustration at right), so that the block surface resting on the base is flat and the lip faces up

Stones positioned on a bank will hold it in place. Set plants in the spaces between rocks.

A MODULAR BLOCK RETAINING WALL

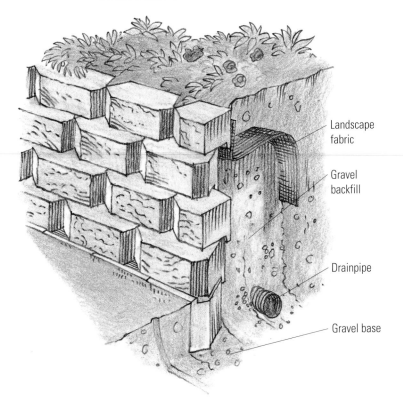

Landscape fabric

Gravel backfill

Drainpipe

Gravel base

This low retaining wall is made from several sizes of split-face concrete blocks that were manufactured to resemble cut stone. A decorative block cap provides the finishing touch.

at the front of the wall. The subsequent rows should be laid with the lip at the rear for proper batter.

With all styles of blocks, stagger the joints as you would for a stone wall. To make the ends of the wall flush, use half blocks if they are available, or cut a block in half with a masonry saw or by scoring the block with a masonry chisel and hitting it sharply with a short-handled sledgehammer or a drilling hammer. Use cap pieces for the top row.

BROKEN CONCRETE

Pieces of broken-up sidewalks or concrete slabs may be used like stone. The chunks look surprisingly natural when laid dry in courses with the rough surface facing up and the smooth side down. Break any large sections into pieces small enough to handle; an electric jackhammer is a better tool for the job than a sledgehammer, which tends to shatter the concrete. As with stone walls, stagger the joints when you build the wall.

MORTARED WALLS

Brick and stone are suitable materials for low mortared retaining walls, and concrete block is a good choice for taller walls or unstable hillsides. You can construct mortared stone walls up to about a foot tall on well-compacted soil. Taller mortared walls of all types require a large concrete footing. You may want to hire a contractor to build the footing for a brick or stone retaining wall, then construct the actual wall yourself. A concrete block wall, from the footing up, typically is a job for a contractor.

BRICK

Brick retaining walls more than 1 foot tall are usually built with double rows of bricks, called wythes, for extra strength. Even so, the small size of each unit and the consequent large number of mortar joints make brick a sound material for retaining walls only up to about 2 feet tall. You can extend this limit somewhat with steel reinforcing rods embedded in grout between the double rows of bricks (see at bottom left). However, most brick retaining walls built today—short as well as tall ones—usually consist of brick veneered onto half-thick, steel-reinforced concrete block.

STONE

Mortared stone walls are stronger than those made of brick. You may use almost any kind of stones, including round ones. Once the footing is installed, building a mortared wall is similar to erecting a dry-stone wall. Dry-fit the stones before spreading the mortar bed, and fill large gaps with small stones. Clean up spilled mortar from the face of the stone with a wet sponge as you work.

CONCRETE BLOCK

This type of retaining wall is less expensive than one made of poured concrete, but it's nearly as strong. Unless you have building expertise, hire a qualified contractor to build the block wall, reinforcing it as necessary to meet the building department's specifications.

POURED CONCRETE WALLS

A steel-reinforced cast-concrete wall is the strongest type of retaining wall, but it's generally not a job for a do-it-yourselfer, and the formwork and labor for a large wall can make it a costly project. Still, it may be the best solution for a difficult hillside. A concrete wall needn't be plain: lining the forms with rough-sawn lumber or using an exposed-aggregate finish can add surface interest. Or you can apply a brick or stone veneer to the surface (see opposite page).

REINFORCING A BRICK WALL

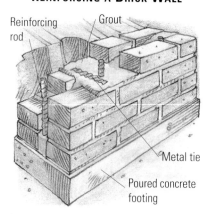

Reinforcing rod
Grout
Metal tie
Poured concrete footing

A simple way to strengthen a brick retaining wall is to pour grout—thin, soupy concrete—between the wythes. Once it has stiffened slightly, insert steel rods into the grout right down to the footing; or place steel rods in the footing when it is poured and build around them, then add grout to the cavity between the wythes. To stabilize the wall further, use metal ties every couple of courses.

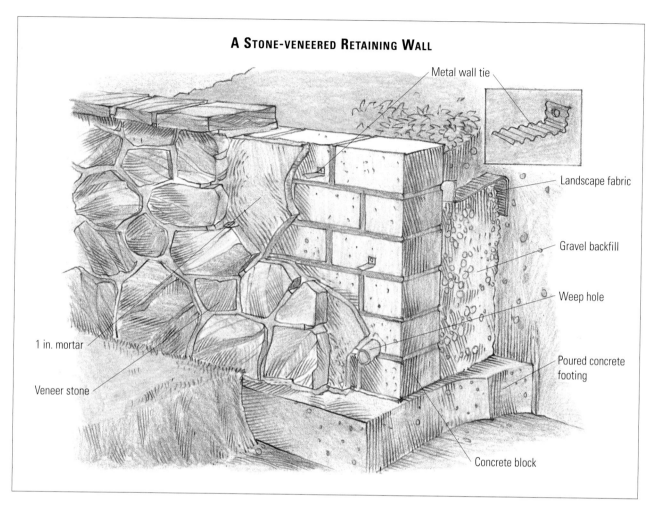

A STONE-VENEERED RETAINING WALL

Metal wall tie

Landscape fabric

Gravel backfill

Weep hole

Poured concrete footing

Concrete block

1 in. mortar

Veneer stone

VENEERED WALLS

Concrete block or poured concrete retaining walls—either existing or newly built—may be faced with stone or brick for a more attractive look. While it's best to have an experienced contractor build such walls, you may do the veneering yourself if you wish.

Excavate to the footing of an existing wall. Clean the surface of the wall and footing, then allow the concrete to dry before proceeding further. Use masonry nails to attach noncorrosive metal wall ties about 2 to 3 feet apart. On an existing concrete-block wall, nail the ties into the blocks—not the joints. On a new wall, ties should be inserted into the mortar joints of every other row of blocks as the wall is built. Allow a newly poured concrete retaining wall to cure before affixing ties.

Mortar the bricks or stones to the wall, starting from the footing and working upward. For a brick facade, use veneer brick, which is thinner than standard brick; it may be laid in any number of patterns. Bricks set on edge form an attractive cap. Veneer stone is cut to a uniform thickness; when applying it to a wall, face the rougher side outward. Unless the stones have been at least roughly squared, it won't be possible to lay them in horizontal courses; you'll need to build an agreeable arrangement of irregular shapes. For an interesting pattern, choose a range of sizes. Place the largest stones at the base of the wall and orient every stone as it might lie naturally on the ground—not on end or in an obviously unnatural position. Place a stone over the juncture of two, as you would if building a wall completely of stone. Use large, flat stones on top of the wall to form a cap.

Veneer stone was mortared to the surface of this poured concrete wall to give it a more decorative look. The veneering is evident at the stairway opening, where you can see the stone does not continue up the stairwell wall.

PLANTING BEDS AND TERRACES

Rather than plant on the slant, create level beds to simplify planting and maintenance. Raised beds framed with wood, stone, or other materials are suitable for most slopes. On modest inclines, you may want to forgo framing in favor of open terraces. Both types of beds will slow the rush of water downhill, thus reducing erosion and allowing moisture to get to plant roots. It's also a cinch to work organic matter into level beds, making them especially useful for vegetable and flower gardens.

PLANNING AHEAD

Consider which type of planting areas will work best on your terrain. Should they be informal, open terraces or structured, framed beds? If the latter is more suitable, choose a construction material that is compatible with the rest of your landscape. Unless you already have access to the new planting areas, you'll also need paths (and likely steps) to get there, plus some way to get to the individual beds or terraces to plant and maintain them.

Limit the size of each planting area to about 3 feet across if you can reach in from only one side, 4 feet if you can access it from opposite sides. To help you visualize the beds, outline their proposed borders with stakes and string. If you're unhappy with the results, simply remove the markings and start again.

Remember, when building tiers of open terraces or raised beds, start at the bottom of the slope and work upward. That way, you will be building each tier atop a firm foundation.

OPEN TERRACES

Think of unframed terraces as broad, deep steps that are dug in for a stairway but on a grander scale. Cut into the existing slope and use excavated soil as fill. You can form a low soil berm at the front edge of each terrace to slow the downhill flow of water.

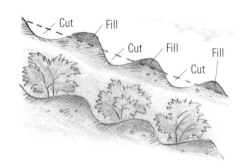

FRAMED RAISED BEDS

These beds—or framed terraces—are typically 1 to 2 feet tall. In a way they are like little retaining walls, but they don't require such careful engineering unless they're on steep or unstable hillsides. On gentle slopes, they may be casual surrounds just sturdy enough to hold plantings and soil in place.

The easiest raised beds to build are made from stackable materials such as railroad ties or landscape timbers, rocks, broken chunks of concrete, or modular concrete

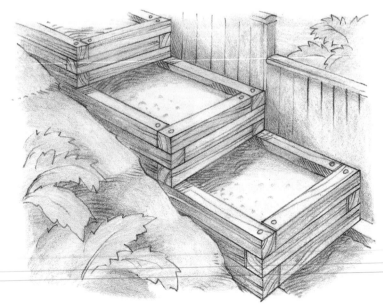

STAIR-STEP TIMBER TERRACES

This design uses the rear of each bed as the foundation for the next one. Dig a trench to accommodate the front and side walls of the lowest terrace. Compact and level the soil in the trench, then position the timbers. Drill holes in the ends of the timbers to accept galvanized steel pipe or reinforcing bar; pound the anchors into the ground. Position the next row of timbers directly on top of the first, staggering the corners; connect the timbers to the bottom row with spikes. Repeat for any additional rows.

For the next bed, cut into the slope and transfer the excavated soil into the first bed. (If you plan to fill the beds with an improved soil mix, use the excavated soil as fill elsewhere.) Position the bottom timbers for the second bed so they overlap the side walls of the lower bed and build the second terrace as you did the first. Build additional beds as desired. When you get to the last bed, make a back wall of timbers that is level with the front wall of that bed.

Fieldstones form a series of simple, casual planting terraces on a gentle bank. The top and bottom terraces consist of small, dry-stacked stones, while the intermediate ones contain larger rocks next to each other. The emphasis is on informality: tight joints in stacked rows aren't necessary—the odd rock that tumbles out of place is easily restored.

blocks. Building raised beds from dimensional lumber is also a fairly easy project for the do-it-yourselfer. Whatever your choice, be sure the framing material is sturdy enough and sufficiently anchored to remain in place through downpours or, in cold climates, freezes and thaws. Both casual and more carefully engineered raised beds will last for many years if built on compacted and leveled soil. Large framed terraces should be treated like full-fledged retaining walls, and special attention should be paid to proper drainage (see page 100).

BOULDER TERRACE

For a terraced planting area that looks completely natural, position large rocks on a slope and secure them by partially burying the base of each stone. Fill in behind the rocks with soil, then plant.

WOOD BEDS

Framing options include railroad ties, landscape timbers, logs, and boards. For the longest-lasting frames, choose lumber that is rot resistant (redwood, cedar, or cypress) or pressure treated. You may build a stand-alone bed or a series of beds that ascends the slope. For greatest stability, anchor the beds as for retaining walls made of the same type of lumber (see page 102). The easiest way to secure landscape logs is to stake them in front.

STONE SURROUNDS

Natural stone is an attractive material that's easy to stack into walls for a raised bed; the look of the bed will depend on the size and shape of the stones. Walls lower than 2 feet tall don't need mortar or footings. For greater stability, fit the stones together carefully so that the edges of some nestle into the crannies of others. Stagger the joints from one tier of stones to the next.

CONCRETE BEDS

You can stack broken pieces of concrete as you would natural stone; for the most attractive appearance, expose the rough surfaces. Modular concrete blocks offer another sure-fire option for the do-it-yourselfer. These are the precast, interlocking blocks developed for retaining walls (see page 103).

The flat stones that make up these rather formal-looking, mortared beds serve several purposes: they enclose the beds, serve as steps and paths to the plants, and provide seating.

DECKS

On hilly terrain, a deck is often the only way to create a large, level outdoor living space. While a patio may be limited by topography, a deck can defy it, floating over steep slopes or stepping down by connecting platforms into the landscape. Many hillside properties offer splendid views, and what better place to enjoy them than from a deck? If planting space is scarce on a very steep or inaccessible site, beds may be incorporated into the deck design.

BUILDING CODES

Most municipalities require a permit for decks over a certain height or square footage, so check with your local building department at the beginning of the project. Codes govern many aspects of deck construction, including the depth of footings, size of beams, fastening techniques, and type of bracing. Decks on steep slopes typically need structural engineering and special building department approval. Where landslides may occur, the slope will probably have to be checked by a soils engineer before you can proceed further.

PLANNING

You'll need a plan of the proposed deck, not only to obtain a building permit but also to figure out how much lumber and other materials to buy. A rough sketch is fine if the deck is a do-it-yourself project.

You may prefer to work with a professional deck designer or builder, especially for a complicated or elaborate deck or one situated on an unstable or steep hillside. Keep in mind that the higher off the ground the deck is, generally the harder it is to build. When the deck floor is more than about 6 feet above ground level, it's difficult to position posts, beams, and other framing elements. Deck building can also be risky business when you're trying to balance tools or steady a ladder on sloping ground.

Deck construction must take many factors into account. The load that a deck must carry—meaning the weight of the structural components, as well as the weight of people, movable deck furniture, and (in wintry climates) snow accumulation—must be computed, and the deck built to withstand that stress. If the deck must carry an abnormally heavy load, such as a large number of soil-filled planters, special reinforcement

When a deck is cantilevered—extended beyond its support posts—over a steep hillside, it looks as if it's floating over the landscape.

may be needed. Different formulas are used to determine the size and number or spacing of the various deck components. For example, the greater the number of footings, the smaller the beams can be. The larger the deck, the bigger and closer together the joists must be. Fortunately, if you do decide to tackle the deck construction yourself, most lumberyards and home centers can help you if you provide them with dimensions and plans.

FOOTINGS

These concrete bases are your deck's first line of support, and their placement, size, and depth are important, particularly on slopes. To ensure that the deck doesn't sink, the footings must rest on firm soil, not fill.

Establishing the exact location of each footing is crucial if all the parts of the deck are to connect securely. Your plan should indicate how far from the house each footing lies and the lateral distances between footings. You'll need mason's line and a line level to measure distances to footings; use a plumb bob suspended from the string to transfer the measurement to ground level.

Dig each footing hole to the required size and depth; there may be several different dimensions for a hillside deck. A manual or power posthole digger may be adequate for excavating holes on gentle or moderate slopes. On steep hills, you may have to hire a professional to drill footing holes with an auger attached to a truck or tractor drilling rig.

Sometimes a footing is set entirely below ground and a separate pier is placed on top of it to elevate the deck post above grade and protect it from rot. A precast concrete pier is adequate for low decks in areas where the ground doesn't freeze. For hillside decks or in cold-winter areas, a pier cast on site in a purchased fiber form or homemade wooden form placed atop the footing is stronger. Often, the footing and pier are cast as a single unit that is referred to simply as a footing. For decks perched on steep hillsides, a footing may take the form of a reinforced concrete column.

POSTS

On level terrain, posts will be a uniform height, but on a hillside, post height will vary, often dramatically. The tops of the posts must be level with each other, even when their bottoms aren't.

Cut each post longer than its estimated finished length. Temporarily set it in place on its footing, then plumb and level it. Use mason's line and a line level to mark each post even with the top of the ledger (a plank or beam connecting the deck to the house wall), which creates a base elevation for the deck; or use a water level (see page 115) between the ledger and the deck post. If the design calls for a beam to rest on the post, subtract the beam's depth and make a new mark. Remove the post and cut it to the correctly marked height.

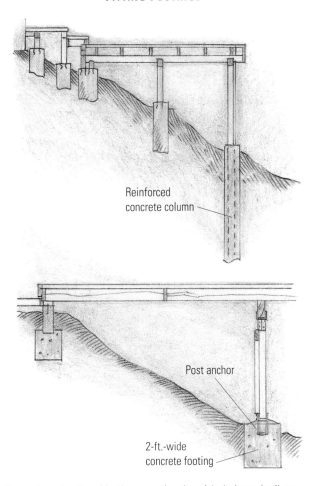

Reinforced concrete column

Post anchor

2-ft.-wide concrete footing

Size and construction of footings are a function of deck size and soil conditions; your local building code may impose certain requirements as well. On a steep or unstable slope, extra-deep concrete columns with reinforcing bar may be appropriate (top), or the situation may call for wider but shallower supports (bottom).

MEASURING DECK POSTS

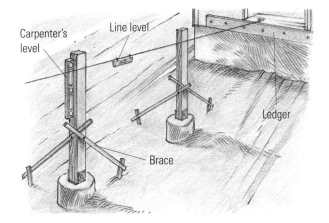

Carpenter's level

Line level

Ledger

Brace

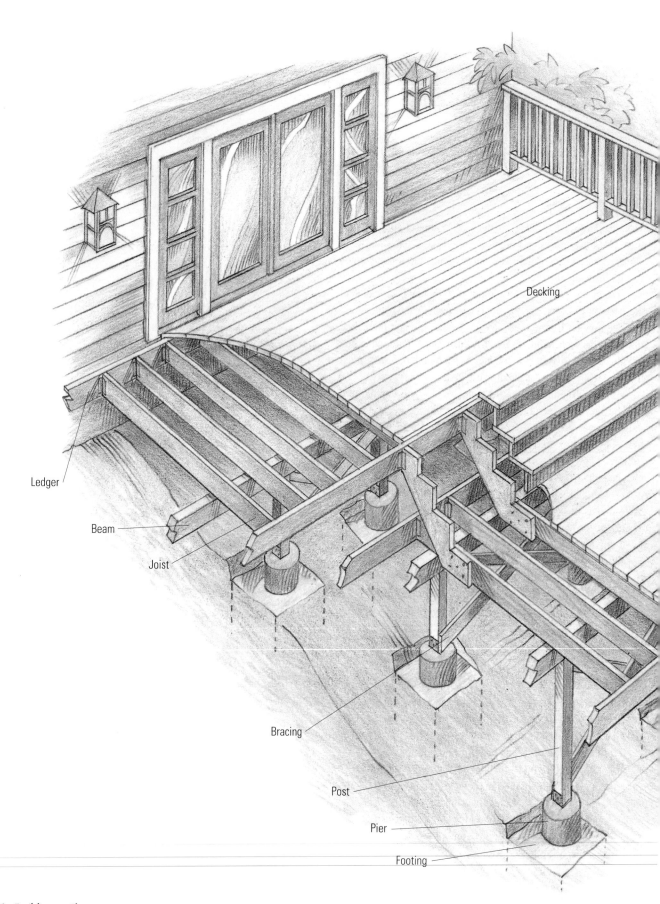

Decking

Ledger

Beam

Joist

Bracing

Post

Pier

Footing

ANATOMY OF A DECK

The foundation—footings and piers—supports a substructure of posts, beams, and joists. Decking is nailed over the substructure to form the finished floor; you may want to consider synthetic decking, which is longer lasting and easier to maintain than wood. A ledger connects the deck to the house.

ON-DECK GARDENING

On hillsides where planting space is limited or hard to reach, a large deck such as this one built on a rooftop provides a convenient place to garden. Remember, the added weight of soil-filled containers must be taken into account when constructing any deck, especially one located on a roof.

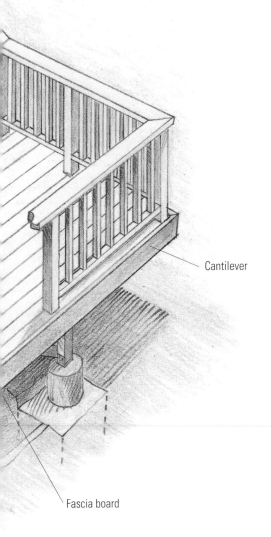

Cantilever

Fascia board

BUILDING AROUND A TREE

Opening to allow for tree growth

A tree can add beauty and shade to your deck, so think twice before cutting down a handsome specimen that happens to be in your planned deck-building area. You can build a deck around a tree without disturbing its roots. Remember to allow space for the trunk to grow and to sway in the wind. Never attach any lumber to the trunk—it will harm the tree, and the tree's movement in wind will damage the deck.

PATIOS AND SITTING PLACES

A patio should be an inviting spot for outdoor relaxation. If it will also serve as a dining area, look for a site conveniently close to the house and choose a smooth patio surface so tables and chairs won't wobble. When traipsing up and down slopes, you'll also appreciate resting spots along the way. These may be little patios or strategically placed store-bought garden benches or chairs—or something more whimsical, such as seating fashioned from boulders.

PLACING A PATIO

Finding just the right flat space (or easily leveled spot) for a patio can be difficult on some hillside lots. Your choices may be limited, but strive for a comfortable exposure and a good view. (If the view is disagreeable, be sure it can be screened with plants or structures.) Situate the patio close to the house if there's room, or choose the flattest area elsewhere in the garden, keeping in mind that you may not use your "outdoor room" if it's too far away. For drainage, the patio floor should actually slant 1 to 2 percent (a drop of ⅛ to ¼ inch for every foot of distance), but it will still look flat.

Remember, a patio doesn't have to be a neat square, rectangle, or semicircle; it can curve and jut as needed to take advantage of available space. You can cut into a hillside to expand the patio area, but don't build on top of fill unless you work with a professional to secure the filled area. On a gentle slope, you may prefer to limit excavation and instead create two or more patio levels connected by steps.

Paving over tree roots may irreparably damage some trees. If you can't avoid placing the patio over a tree's root zone, choose a permeable paving, such as bricks on sand or flagstones in soil, so air and water can get to the roots.

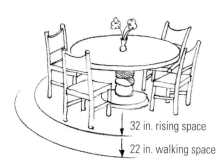

↓ 32 in. rising space
↓ 22 in. walking space

Allow at least 4½ feet of clearance all around a patio table, especially one used for dining.

PAVING MATERIALS

The most common materials for patio floors are brick, stone, interlocking concrete pavers, and poured concrete—the latter in the form of a single large slab or individual small slabs.

A poured concrete patio is usually a job for a professional, but bricks, stones, and concrete pavers are easy for do-it-yourselfers to work with. These masonry units can be set on a 2-inch bed of sand with an edging to retain it (path edgings described on page 98 are suitable for patios). Where rains are heavy or the ground freezes in winter, install 4 to 8 inches of gravel beneath the sand to stabilize the patio and improve drainage. Set the masonry units, tapping them into place with a rubber mallet and leveling them as you go. When the patio is laid, sweep sand into the joints and sprinkle water over the patio to settle the sand. As an alternative, fill the spaces with dry mortar, then moisten the patio; the filled joints will harden. This method requires careful sweeping because any mortar left on the surface will adhere to the masonry.

The various masonry units may be set in mortar on a concrete pad rather than on a sand base, although this job requires more expertise. If the pad must be constructed, you'll probably want to hire a contractor experienced in building forms and pouring concrete, but if you have a concrete slab that just needs rejuvenation, you may want to take on the task of mortaring bricks, stones, or pavers to the surface yourself.

On a hillside lot, the best plan is to throw out any notions of an ideal patio site or configuration and work with available level space, even if it's away from the house or an odd shape. This small patio—made of flagstone set in soil with creeping plants between the pavers—provides a picturesque spot to relax and contemplate nature.

BRICK

Common brick is better suited to patios than face brick because its surface is rougher and provides more traction. Standard bricks are used on a sand base. Paver bricks, which are about half the thickness of standard bricks, are used on top of a concrete pad. Outdoor bricks are graded according to their ability to withstand weathering; if you live in a region where it regularly freezes and thaws, be sure to use the appropriate product. More than color, texture, or size, the pattern in which the bricks are laid is what makes a brick patio interesting.

STONE

Flagstone—any flat stone that's either naturally thin or split from a rock that cleaves easily—is a popular choice for patios. Many colors and textures are available; choices tend to vary by region. Flagstone sold for paving is usually 1 to 2 inches thick; for the most stable paving surface, select large pieces at the thick end of the range. To keep chairs and tables steady, look for stones with a fairly smooth surface.

As an alternative to setting flagstones in sand or mortar, you may set them directly in tamped soil, with plantings between the stones, for a natural look. Before you start constructing the patio, lay out the stones and rearrange them as needed until you are satisfied. Remember, the stones are heavy—you'll need help positioning them.

Many stone types, including slate, sandstone, granite, limestone, and travertine, are available precut in rectangular tiles. Cut stone is usually laid in mortar with thin grout lines, although heavier tiles may be laid on sand.

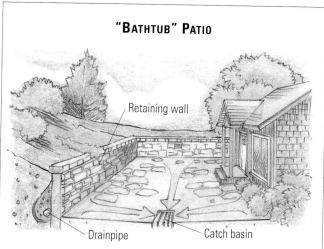

"BATHTUB" PATIO

Retaining wall

Drainpipe   Catch basin

When building a patio between the house and a retaining wall, slope the patio floor toward a drain so it empties like a bathtub (see "Catch basin" on page 89). Also, install a drainpipe behind the retaining wall to carry subsurface water away.

INTERLOCKING CONCRETE PAVERS

Although these pavers are made of concrete, many are textured and colored to resemble stone, adobe, or other materials. The pavers come in circles, squares, rectangles, and various custom shapes. They fit together like jigsaw puzzle pieces, forming a surface more rigid than one made of brick; single pavers can't tip out of alignment as individual bricks can.

POURED CONCRETE

A concrete patio doesn't have to be a boring gray rectangle. Flexible wooden forms can be used to define a freeform slab, while rigid forms can create different geometric shapes. Color-dusting, staining, sandblasting, rock-salting, and acid-washing are other ways to add character. The concrete may also be tinted and stamped to mimic stone, tile, or brick. Another way to soften the look of a concrete slab is to incorporate planting pockets in it.

Although a poured concrete patio is usually a job for a professional, creating one that resembles flagstone in soil can be a do-it-yourself project. Use the same technique as you would for concrete stepping-stones (see page 98), starting by arranging torn pieces of newspaper on the ground in the patio shape of your choice. Make the surface of the individual concrete slabs fairly smooth so that tables and chairs will sit solidly. Plant between the concrete slabs after they've cured.

INFORMAL SEATING

Your landscape may have few level tracts, but you can still provide places to sit and rest. Place a purchased garden bench along a pathway or build your own there—like this natural-looking one consisting of a flat stone slab laid across two round boulders.

There are other ways to incorporate seating into the landscape. If you're building raised beds, include a wide cap for seating. Let a large, flat-topped rock serve double duty as an accent and a seat. Or incorporate extra-wide steps into stairs—people can stop and rest or chat without impeding others moving along the stairway.

FENCES AND GATES

A hillside poses no barrier to building a fence, although you'll have to construct one differently than you would on level ground. The fence may follow the slope's natural contours—or step down the hillside in a series of level sections. Even a gate is no problem if you arrange hinges and swing direction to avoid a collision with the slope.

CONTOURED OR STEPPED FENCE?

There are two basic fence styles that can be built along a hillside. A contoured fence runs parallel to the slope, with the rails and siding following the contour of the land. A stepped fence is laid out in level sections like stairs.

A contoured fence is easier to build and works on almost any slope and even along bumpy terrain, but you may prefer the appearance of a stepped fence, especially when the fence is viewed in direct relationship to the house. A contoured fence tends to look lopsided against straight, architectural lines; that's not an issue when the fence is seen in the context of the landscape.

Designs that adapt especially well to contoured fencing include post-and-rail fences and solid fences using pickets, palings, or grape stakes. Wire field fencing and vinyl post-and-rail fences that parallel the slope are often used on rural properties. Stepped fences are a good solution for board, louver, basketweave, and panel fences. Choose a design that complements your house and setting.

PLANNING AHEAD

Before you make specific plans for the size, style, and location of your fence, check with your local building department about any required setbacks or restrictions on fence height or material. There may be a rule dictating that the "good side" of the fence (the side to which the siding is affixed) face the neighboring property. For lumber fences, be sure to choose decay-resistant (redwood, cedar, or cypress) or pressure-treated wood, just as you would for a wood retaining wall or raised planting beds.

A fence built on the property line belongs to you and the owners of the adjoining land, even if they don't contribute to its cost or maintenance. If you intend a boundary fence to be your own, build it a foot or so within your property to be safe. If you can't find out where the property line is, have the land surveyed rather than take the chance of building the fence in the wrong place.

If the fence is to go along a bank or cliff, it's a good idea to consult a landscape architect or engineer first. A retaining wall may be necessary, or you may simply have to anchor the posts a specified depth below shifting soil.

CONTOURED POST-AND-RAIL FENCE

CONTOURED PICKET FENCE

STEPPED POST-AND-RAIL FENCE

STEPPED BOARD FENCE

PLOTTING THE FENCE

The first step in building a fence is to locate the exact course it will take and mark the line with stakes and string. You can easily plot it yourself if the slope is gradual and uniform, with no large humps or depressions along the fence line. You may decide to have a professional lay out and build a fence running along a very steep or irregular slope.

FOLLOWING THE SLOPE

For a contoured fence, mark the fence line by driving end stakes and stretching mason's line between them; the line should be tied to the stakes at a set distance off the ground and high enough to clear the ground and any plantings. For rolling or uneven terrain, you may need to tie the line to intermediate stakes.

To determine the number of posts you'll need, measure the fence distance along the string line; then, using the maximum post spacing of 8 feet, divide the total fence distance by 8. If the resulting number ends in a fraction, round up to the next whole number. Divide the total distance by that whole number to get the exact spacing between posts (the distance from the center of one post to the center of the next post).

Measure and mark the post locations on the string. Then, use a plumb bob to transfer the marks you made on the string to the ground beneath —for example, by driving nails through pieces of paper.

STEPPING DOWN

For a stepped fence, drive the end stakes, using a tall stake at the downhill end so its top is at about the same elevation as the top of the uphill end stake. Mark a point 6 inches from the ground on the uphill stake and hold one end of a water level alongside the stake so that the water levels off at the mark (you can make your own level by taping clear plastic tubing to each end of an ordinary garden hose). Enlist a helper to hold that end of the water level in place while you hold the other end against the downhill stake. When the water finds its level, mark that point.

Measure down from this point to the ground, then subtract 6 inches to get the height differential of the slope—2½ feet in this example. Measure the distance of the fence line

FOLLOWING THE SLOPE

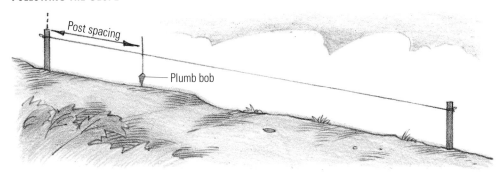

Post spacing

Plumb bob

STEPPING DOWN

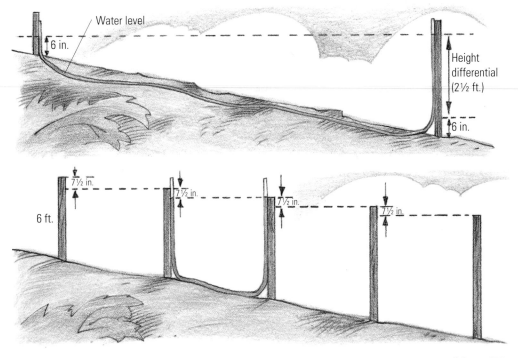

Water level

6 in.

Height differential (2½ ft.)

6 in.

7½ in.

7½ in.

7½ in.

7½ in.

6 ft.

and determine the post spacing and the consequent number of fence sections as you would for a contoured fence. Convert the height differential of the slope to inches and divide by the number of fence sections to find the amount of drop per section. For example, a 30-inch height differential divided by four fence sections results in a 7½-inch drop per section.

Mark the post locations as for a contoured fence. Set the post at the uphill end of the fence to the desired height (6 feet in the example on page 115). Measure the amount of the drop (7½ inches) from the top of the post and mark it on the side facing the next post. Hold one end of a water level at the mark on the first post and the other end against the second post set loosely in place. When the water finds its level, mark that point on the second post to indicate the final height of that post. Continue this process with the successive posts.

CONSTRUCTING THE FENCE

The most important part of fence building is setting the posts. They must be located precisely in line and plumb in their holes or you'll encounter difficulties when adding the rails and siding. The posts must also be firmly set in the ground to ensure the fence is stable (see the illustration below).

Posthole depth depends on fence height and soil texture. Generally, you should set posts about 1½ to 2 feet deep, deeper for taller fences and for lighter or sandier soils. Where the ground freezes, dig below the frost line.

Setting and aligning posts is best done by two people—one to hold and align the post with a level while the other fills the hole with concrete. Ready-mix concrete simplifies the job of setting posts. You may mix the concrete with water before shoveling it

CONCRETE CONNECTIONS

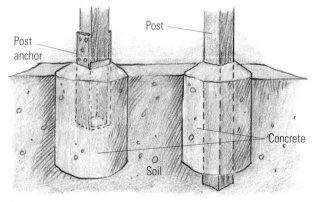

For the longest-lasting posts, keep them entirely above the ground by attaching them to post anchors set in concrete (left). If you set posts directly in concrete, use a concrete collar with the end of each post protruding into soil (right), rather than encased completely in concrete or sitting on gravel, so moisture isn't trapped against it. In the two examples illustrated here, the concrete is sloped at the top so water sheds away from the posts instead of pooling around the wood.

DESIGNING A GATE

Make gates a minimum of 3 feet wide (3½ or 4 feet is better) to accommodate a wheelbarrow or garden cart. Build a rectangular frame, making sure that each of the four corners forms a 90-degree angle. You may cut the siding to follow the slope if you hinge the gate on the downhill side; it may be hinged to swing in either direction. A gate that sits perpendicular to the slope (across the slope rather than along it) must be hinged to swing downhill.

Siding cut to follow slope

into the hole (be sure to "rod" the wet concrete by plunging a rod or dowel into it to release air bubbles and compact the mix) or, even easier, pour dry concrete into the hole and dribble in water.

When the posts are firmly set in their holes, the next step is to install the rails, or stringers, and the siding. The top and bottom rails form the framework to which the siding is attached. On a contoured fence, the rails run parallel to the ground. On a typical stepped fence, they are level and parallel to each other but not to the ground.

The method you use to fasten the rails to the posts depends on the fence design and the materials chosen. The various techniques include butting the rails between the posts, recessing the rails into the posts by means of dadoes or notches, lapping the rails over the sides or tops of the posts, and passing the rails through mortises in the posts.

Attaching the siding to the rails will go faster with two people—one to hold the siding in place and another to do the fastening. Use galvanized nails or screws to affix the siding. Plan on cutting the bottom ends of fence boards on the slant to follow hill contours; cutting them straight would leave triangular gaps between the fence and hill. On a stepped fence with panels that can't be cut on the slant, you could fill the spaces with additional lumber—or choose a different design to avoid creating gaps.

In this multilevel waterfall, the water source is hidden and carefully placed rocks divide the gush of water into separate cascades.

WATER FEATURES

Waterfalls, flowing streams, and dry creekbeds are often difficult to incorporate into flat terrain without looking contrived, but they blend beautifully into hillside landscapes. They look most authentic running along natural contours, such as when a waterfall spills off a rock ledge, or a stream or dry creekbed follows a gully. In a hillside garden, a water feature may also be functional, by directing seasonal runoff. Before you start building, lay out the feature (with rope, a garden hose, or water-soluble spray paint) to be sure the shape is pleasing.

WATERFALLS

A hillside landscape offers many opportunities to showcase falling water. You may break the fall into stages, or stair steps, or have the water drop all at once in a dramatic plunge. Inspect your property for just the right waterfall site; as you survey various inclines and outcroppings, try to imagine what they will look like with water coursing down.

A constructed waterfall works like this: The water drops over carefully placed rocks into a pond or other reservoir set in a fairly level area (unless you plan for it to cascade into a running stream or other watercourse). A small pump sits in the pond; plastic tubing attached to it recirculates water back to a reservoir at the top of the falls. If there is no upper reservoir and the water is routed to just above the stone over which the water falls, it will gush over the top and not drop properly. The upper reservoir needn't be large, and concealing it makes for a more natural-looking waterfall.

A waterfall derives most of its character from the placement of rocks. Typically, there are several main stones augmented by any number of smaller ones. The water usually falls over a spill stone (also referred to as a mirror stone). The stone's shape and the texture of its lip determine the pattern of the fall. A wide, rectangular stone with a smooth lip produces a neat curtain of water, while a narrow stone with a jagged lip creates streams of water.

The spill stone may be cantilevered over a backing stone. A small groove, or reglet, cut on the underside of the spill stone will prevent water from dripping back and spoiling the effect of the fall. Instead of a spill stone, you could position two stones on either side of the channel at the edge of the falls and leave a gap in the middle—a weir—through which the water flows and drops to the level below.

A relatively short waterfall may feature a spill stone flanked by large vertical stones that lean slightly inward toward the channel. These may be stabilized by smaller stones at their base. For a taller cascade, or one that descends in steps, choose a variety of large and smaller stones to edge the channel. If you place a large stone in the lower pond, the falling water will rush against it, creating interesting sounds. The stone will also deflect the force of the falling water, reducing the splash and bubbling-up effects.

There are no firm rules for the number, size, and placement of the stones. The key is experimentation—moving a rock here, a rock there—until the waterfall looks and sounds its best. Remember, the falls should also look good when the water is turned off.

BUILDING THE FALLS

Waterproofing the entire structure—upper and lower reservoirs and falls—is crucial, to make sure water doesn't escape and soil doesn't wash into the lower pool. Choose a flexible liner, freeform concrete, a fiberglass shell or series of spill pans, or a combination of these materials. Professionals often use a flexible liner underneath concrete; the liner provides insurance against leaks in the concrete while allowing you the freedom to sculpt the channel with

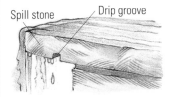

REGULATING THE FLOW

Spill stone   Drip groove

A groove on the underside of the spill stone keeps water from dripping backward and ruining the effect of the waterfall.

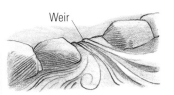

Weir

Instead of having a spill stone, you could arrange for water to flow through a gap called a weir. Its size and shape control the flow of water out of the upper reservoir.

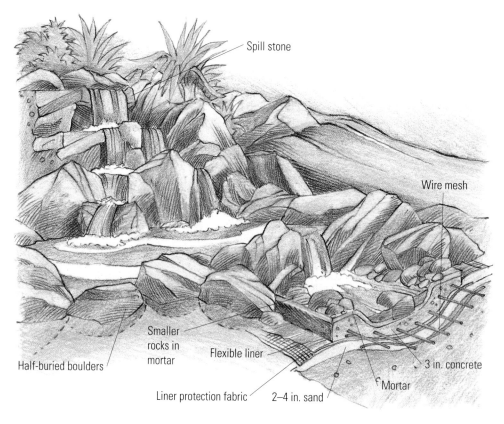

Spill stone

Wire mesh

Smaller rocks in mortar

Half-buried boulders

Flexible liner

3 in. concrete

Mortar

Liner protection fabric

2–4 in. sand

concrete and set rocks in mortar. You'll need steel reinforcement—either reinforcing bar or wire mesh—for concrete channels. Take care not to puncture the liner when pouring the concrete.

Dig out the reservoirs at the top and base of the waterfall and compact the soil, being sure to slope the pools slightly from front to back. You'll build these structures first, then connect the falls to the pools.

The toughest part of the project is maneuvering any big boulders into place. If you're using a flexible liner, position these rocks carefully, making sure not to damage or displace the liner. If the rocks are outside the liner's path, dig out beds and settle them firmly in the soil. You may need to hire someone with specialized equipment to position very large stones, which must be securely set so that they don't move and crack the waterproofing.

Once the basic structure is complete, secure the secondary stones, pebbles, and spill stone in a mortar bed. Colored mortar—black or charcoal—blends in better than natural gray, appearing as shadows in the finished waterfall. Add loose rocks or pebbles as a visual accent or to form ripple patterns. To secure border plantings, pack soil into areas behind the boulders.

FLOWING STREAMS

You may build a streambed that flows from an artificial spring or one that channels water between a waterfall and pond. Build it along a mild slope and be sure the proposed channel can handle the maximum flow from your pump, plus some additional natural runoff. The difference between a streambed meant to hold flowing water and a dry creekbed (see at right) is that the streambed must be waterproofed like a waterfall.

CONSTRUCTING A STREAM

Start by laying out the streambed, giving it curves and bends along the way. Make the stream broad enough to accommodate some rocks in the channel as well as at the edges, but don't make the width uniform. Natural streams widen at bends, leaving promontories on inside curves and eroded banks on outside curves. Figure on a finished depth of 3 to 7 inches for the shallow stretches, 10 inches in the occasional deep pools (water will collect here when the pump is turned off).

You may form a concrete channel, but a flexible liner will do the trick with a lot less work and easier maintenance. In time, concrete channels tend to develop cracks and leaks that are often hard to trace. Place mixed rocks, pebbles, gravel, and sand in

This small stream, connected to a constructed waterfall on the same property, is lined with boulders and smaller rocks carefully selected for their contours and colors. It contributes to the landscape's general air of tranquillity.

and along the watercourse. Rocks jutting into or randomly distributed in the stream create eddies. Mimic nature: boulders too big to roll in the current remain in the middle of the stream and smaller ones wash to the sides, where they lie half-buried in silt. Turn on the water and experiment with placement of rocks until you like the look and sound of the stream. Finish the edging, disguising the liner with overhanging rocks or a layer of sand or gravel.

DRY CREEKBEDS

This feature is popular in water-conserving and natural landscapes. If it follows a downward grade, it doubles as a drainage channel for seasonal runoff. In fact, you may locate the creekbed along natural depressions and troughs already formed by runoff, or start the creekbed at the "outfall," or open end, of the pipe in a French drain (see page 88); water will funnel into the creekbed during rainstorms. Unlike a stream that is intended to hold water, a dry creekbed doesn't need a waterproof lining since it will be dry most of the time. And letting water soak into the ground during wet weather is usually desirable.

MAKING A DRY CREEKBED

A dry creekbed needs careful planning in order to look realistic. Your challenge is to place the mixed rocks, pebbles, and gravel so as to conjure the idea that the force of water shaped it.

The basic layout is the same as for a flowing stream, except that the bed often contains additional stones to represent flowing water. Excavate the creekbed to the desired depth and width. To use it as a drainage channel, bury a length of 4-inch perforated drainpipe—with the holes facing downward—in the center of the creek.

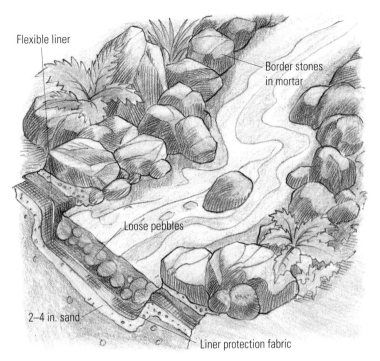

STREAM WITH FLEXIBLE LINER

Flexible liner

Border stones in mortar

Loose pebbles

2–4 in. sand

Liner protection fabric

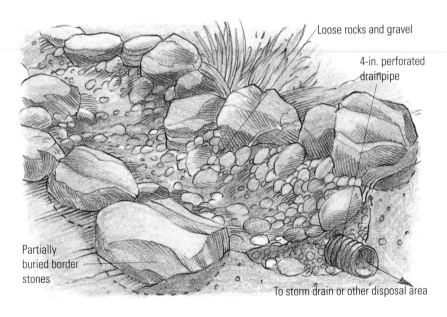

Loose rocks and gravel

4-in. perforated drainpipe

Partially buried border stones

To storm drain or other disposal area

Unless your hillside has been converted into level planting areas with terraces, retaining walls, or raised beds, you'll be growing at least some of your plants on the incline. On a gentle bank, you may plant as if you were on flat ground—but on a moderate or steep slope, you must take special care to protect the soil from eroding.

FOCUSING ON
PLANTS

Choose plants that are well adapted to life on the slant. This chapter suggests some that are suitable; check with a local nursery for additional plants that will succeed in your area. Also look for low-maintenance species if you want to avoid scrambling around your hillside to perform tasks such as weeding and pruning.

Dig planting holes just big enough to accommodate the plants and set the plants carefully into the hillside so you disturb the surrounding soil as little as possible. Be especially cautious when watering new plantings, to avoid washing away the plants or the soil. As the root systems develop, they'll anchor the plants and help hold the soil together, though wise watering practices are still in order to preserve the slope.

Erosion-controlling white clover *(Trifolium repens)* covers this hillside, which features rows of wisteria trained against posts set in low stone walls.

Slope-holding plants, such as the common orange daylily *(Hemerocallis fulva)* set among boulders, succeeded in stopping washouts of this hillside.

CHOOSING PLANTS

For any garden—sloping or flat—you should select plants that appeal to you and that are adapted to your climate and growing conditions. For a hillside garden, you must also consider whether a plant is suited to slope culture—and the steeper the slope, the more attention you must pay to the plant's suitability.

Some plants are good choices for hillsides because they quickly develop a network of dense or wide-spreading roots that knit the soil together and keep it from slipping. Others have branches that put down roots where they touch the ground, creating footholds that stabilize the soil. Above ground, the foliage of both types of plants protects the soil by dissipating the force of rain pelting the slope. Many vines whose roots aren't especially pervasive can still shield a slope with a blanket of foliage; you simply plant the vine at the top of a slope and allow it to drape its meandering stems downward.

The steeper the slope, the harder it is to scramble around and tend plants. If getting around your hillside is arduous, narrow your choices to plants that demand little care, such as a mix of low, spreading shrubs that are attractive and grow well with minimum pruning.

In any garden it's tempting to start off with large plants since they make an immediate impact, but young plants in small containers tend to transplant

A Southern California oceanside slope is densely planted with colorful erosion-controlling plants: white and mauve African daisies *(Osteospermum)*, bluish purple pride of Madeira *(Echium candicans)*, and red-orange Cape honeysuckle *(Tecoma capensis)*.

PLANTS FOR HILLSIDES

Here's a short list of plants adapted to slopes; check locally for other good choices. The symbols shown represent exposure and water preferences; note that many plants accept a range of conditions. Exposure: ☀ full sun, ◐ partial shade, ● little or no direct sun. Moisture (once established): ○ little or no water, ◖ moderate water, ◆ regular water.

Vinca minor

GROUND COVERS

Exposure	Moisture	Plant
☀	○	Acacia redolens
☀◐	○◖	Arctostaphylos uva-ursi (Bearberry)
☀	○	Arctotheca calendula (Cape weed)
☀	○◖	Baccharis pilularis (Dwarf coyote brush)
☀	○	Ceanothus, prostrate forms (Wild lilac)
☀	◖	Conradina verticillata (Cumberland rosemary)
◐	◖	Convallaria majalis (Lily-of-the-valley)
☀◐	○◖◆	Coprosma × kirkii
☀	◖	Coronilla varia (Crown vetch)
☀	○◖	Cotoneaster, prostrate forms
☀◐●	◖◆	Euonymus fortunei, prostrate forms
☀◐	◆	Hemerocallis (Daylily)
☀◐	◖◆	Hypericum calycinum (Creeping St. Johnswort)
☀	○◖	Ice plants, many species (except heavy ones like Carpobrotus)
☀◐	○◖◆	Juniperus, prostrate forms (Juniper)
☀	◖	Lantana, prostrate forms

Delosperma cooperi (Ice plant)

Exposure	Moisture	Plant
☀◐●	◆	Liriope (Lily turf)
☀◐	○	Mahonia repens (Creeping mahonia)
☀◐	◖	Microbiota decussata (Siberian carpet cypress)
☀	○◖	Myoporum parvifolium
☀◐	○◖	Oenothera speciosa (Mexican evening primrose)
☀	◖◆	Osteospermum, spreading forms (African daisy)
☀◐	◖	Phlox subulata (Moss pink)
☀	○◖	Rhus aromatica 'Gro-Low' (Fragrant sumac)
☀	○◖	Rosmarinus officinalis, prostrate forms (Rosemary)
☀◐	◆	Trachelospermum (Star jasmine)
☀◐	◆	Trifolium repens (White clover)
☀◐●	○◖	Vinca (Periwinkle)
☀	○◖	Zauschneria (California fuchsia)

VINES

Exposure	Moisture	Plant
☀	◖◆	Bougainvillea
☀	◆	Clematis terniflora (Sweet autumn clematis)
☀◐	◆	Gelsemium sempervirens (Carolina jessamine)
☀◐	◖◆	Hedera (Ivy)
☀◐	◖◆	Lonicera japonica (Japanese honeysuckle)
☀◐	◖	Macfadyena unguis-cati (Cat's claw)
☀◐●	◖	Parthenocissus quinquefolia (Virginia creeper)
☀◐	◆	Rosa wichuraiana (Memorial rose)
☀◐	○	Tecoma capensis (Cape honeysuckle)
☀	○◖	Wisteria

ORNAMENTAL GRASSES

Many species; exposure and watering needs vary

SHRUBS

Exposure	Moisture	Plant
☀◐	○◖	Arctostaphylos (Manzanita)
☀◐	◖◆	Berberis thunbergii (Japanese barberry)
☀	◆	Calluna vulgaris (Scotch heather)
☀	◖◆	Chaenomeles (Flowering quince)
☀	○	Cistus (Rockrose)
☀◐	◆	Cornus alba (Tatarian dogwood)
☀◐	◆	Cornus stolonifera (Redtwig dogwood)
☀	○◖	Echium candicans (Pride of Madeira)
☀◐	◆	Erica (Heath)
☀	○◖	Eriogonum (Wild buckwheat)
☀	◖◆	Forsythia
☀◐	◆	Heteromeles arbutifolia (Toyon)
☀	○◖	Lycium chinense (Matrimony vine)
☀◐●	◖◆	Physocarpus opulifolius (Common ninebark)
☀	◆	Pyracantha (Firethorn)
☀	○◖	Rhus (Sumac)
☀	○◖	Santolina
VARIES BY SPECIES	○◖	Symphoricarpos (Snowberry, coralberry)

Cistus salvifolius

PLANTS FOR RETAINING WALLS

A cascade of flowers or foliage adds charm to any retaining wall—and it can soften a hard-edged wall or mask an ugly one. A great many plants that billow, trail, or hang down are good candidates. Erosion control isn't a prerequisite since the plants will grow in fairly level ground at the top of the wall.

Brilliantly hued lantana tumbles over a brick retaining wall.

To add appeal to a dry wall made from stacked stones or concrete pieces, try planting in the crevices. Many small plants, including most rock garden plants, make good choices. Some suggestions are listed below; see page 123 for an explanation of symbols relating to exposure and water needs.

☼　　◖◗　*Aethionema* (Stonecress)
☼　　◗　*Arabis* (Rockcress)
☼◐　◗　*Aubrieta deltoidea* (Common aubrieta)
☼◐　◗　*Aurinia saxatilis* (Basket-of-gold)
☼◐　◖◗　*Campanula cochlearifolia* (Fairy thimbles)
☼◐　◗　*Chamaemelum nobile* (Chamomile)
☼◐　◗　*Dianthus gratianopolitanus* (Cheddar pink)
☼◐　◗　*Erigeron karvinskianus* (Mexican daisy)
☼◐　◗　*Erodium reichardii* (Cranesbill)
◐●　◗　Ferns, small species
☼◐　◗　*Geranium, small species* (Cranesbill)
☼　　◗　*Gypsophila repens*
☼◐●　◗　*Herniaria glabra* (Green carpet)
☼◐　◗　*Iberis sempervirens* (Evergreen candytuft)
◐●　◗　*Lamium maculatum* (Dead nettle)
☼◐　◖◗　*Lysimachia nummularia* (Creeping Jenny)
☼　　◖◗　*Saponaria ocymoides*
☼◐　◖◗　*Sedum acre* (Goldmoss sedum)
☼◐　◖◗　*Sempervivum* (Houseleek)
☼◐　◗　*Thymus* (Thyme)

Ground morning glory *(Convolvulus sabatius)* spills over a dry rock wall, while Mexican daisy grows in chinks in the wall.

Garden chores are more difficult on sloping ground than on flat terrain, so keep maintenance requirements in mind when choosing plants.
Design: Tom Chakas

Even if you drew up a meticulous planting plan, double-check the spacing when setting plants in the ground so that you leave adequate access for maintenance. Here, the homeowner can step into the planting to weed it.

better. Small plants—for example, in 4-inch or 1-gallon pots—make particularly good sense on hillsides where the soil is rocky, shallow, or hard to dig, because the planting holes can be small. Some hillsides are so hard to excavate by hand that professional landscapers have to jackhammer holes.

Seeds are easiest to plant because of their tiny size, but you must take special care to protect the slope while the seeds germinate and grow. Jute netting can hold the planting in place (see page 126). Some companies will hydroseed large hillsides; they spray a slurry of seeds, fertilizers, soil amendments, mulch, and stabilizing glues that form a protective crust on the slope.

For a list of plants that are especially well suited to hillside gardens, see page 123. Also check local nurseries for choices recommended for your area. Additionally, your local Cooperative Extension Office or water district may publish a list of erosion-controlling plants.

The bottom of each rock on this newly planted landscape was buried to stabilize the rock. The slope was then thickly mulched to protect the soil while the young plants grow. Because the site is gusty, the young trees were staked with two 2 by 2s positioned at right angles to the strongest winds and driven 18 inches into the ground. Although these stakes are tall, they need to be only a foot or so above ground for sufficient anchorage in a windswept site. Staking should be temporary; these 2 by 2s will be removed after about a year.

PLANTING ON SLOPES

Before planting, amend less-than-ideal soil by digging in organic matter—if you can. On many slopes, including steep or rocky ones, you may not have much soil to work with or the soil may slide downhill when you loosen it. In either case, disturb the soil as little as possible.

You may have a similarly difficult time planting. Excavating individual planting pockets big enough to accommodate the root system is easier than trying to till the soil, and it will interfere less with the slope. You may want to build a mound or terrace for a plant to retain water so that it will soak into the root zone (see page 127). Be judicious in the number of mounds you form because a hillside replete with them may look pockmarked.

For good coverage, arrange plants in drifts and groves, staggering rows to prevent water from running in a straight line downhill. When planting vines to cover a bare slope, train some of the stems to grow up the slope for more uniform coverage; pin them in place with U-shaped stakes.

After planting, apply a thick layer of mulch, taking care not to cover plant crowns (the area where the roots and the stem meet). Mulching serves many purposes: it keeps the soil from being compacted by heavy rains, reduces runoff by slow-

Plants spilling over the edges of paths and stairways are appealing, but keep the mature sizes of these plants in mind when placing them so they won't end up blocking the passage or demand constant cutting back.

HOLD IT!

Jute is a biodegradable netting that protects newly planted slopes from erosion until the plants are established. It is typically sold in 4-foot-wide rolls at irrigation supply stores and some nurseries. To install jute, unfurl the rolls so they run across the grade; tamp the netting into direct contact with soil and secure it with special stakes usually sold with the jute. Cut small, X-shaped holes in the netting and set young plants through them into the ground beneath. Jute may also be used to hold seeds in place; after seeding, roll or tamp the netting lightly, then anchor it. You don't have to remove jute—it starts disintegrating in a few months.

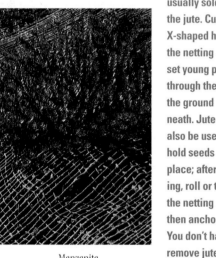

Manzanita (*Arctostaphylos*) was planted through the jute netting.

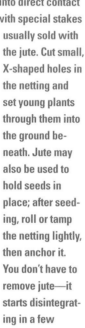

Rather than set all plantings on the incline, you may want to create some level areas for feature plants, as was done here by building retaining walls between the lawn and patio.

ing down the flow of water, conserves soil moisture so plants can go longer between waterings, protects plant roots from excessive heat and cold, and suppresses weeds. Organic mulches such as shredded bark, pine needles, and homemade compost break down slowly, improving the soil and adding nutrients as they decompose; they must be replenished periodically. Choose a mulch that will stay put on your slope; avoid very lightweight materials, which tend to blow away, and rounded ones, such as some bark chips, which may roll downhill.

On a steep slope you may need help in holding soil, plants, and mulch in place until plant roots develop. Jute netting offers an easy way to do this (see at left).

WATERING ON SLOPES

Applied too heavily or too quickly, irrigation water will run off a hillside—not just wasting the water (often before very much of it gets to plant roots), but also eroding the slope. Whether you water by hand or have an automatic irrigation system, you must take care not to apply more moisture than your soil can absorb.

The easiest way to do this is to turn on the water and note how long it takes for runoff to occur, then irrigate just short of that length of time in the future. If enough water does not penetrate to root depth in the allotted time, you can pulse-irrigate: water in short cycles, with rest periods between cycles to allow the moisture to soak in.

Another way to minimize runoff is to slow down the delivery rate of

Drip irrigation devices apply water very slowly, thus limiting runoff. Emitter line, shown here, consists of drip tubing with preinstalled emitters spaced at regular intervals. Unlike a soaker hose, it is clog resistant and works well on slopes.

the water. The output rates of drip emitters, microsprays, emitter line, and other devices associated with low-volume irrigation, or microirrigation, are so slight they are measured in gallons per hour rather than the gallons per minute of traditional sprinklers.

Among traditional sprinklers, rotary heads dispense water more slowly but over a longer distance than spray heads and are sometimes used on large hillsides that don't slope too sharply. If your sprinklers put out too much water too fast, try switching to heads or nozzles that emit less water. Of course, switching to a drip system will drastically reduce the rate at which the water is applied.

When hand-watering, turn the faucet on low. Keep water from running off by directing it into basins you've formed or by using a deep-root irrigator attached to a garden hose. This device injects water into the root zone, shooting it out horizontally in several directions below ground.

Even with a drip or sprinkler irrigation system, basins around plants are handy because they stop or slow the downward flow of any excess water, giving it more time to soak in. You may want to limit basins to large plants with big root systems, to avoid disfiguring the entire hillside.

Microsprays water a planting of mixed ground covers growing on a slope. They apply water much more slowly than do conventional sprinklers, thereby lessening the likelihood of runoff.

AVERTING RUNOFF

Plants on slopes are often challenging to irrigate because water may run downhill faster than it seeps into the root zone. Try building basins and terraces to channel water directly to plant roots. You may build at planting time or "retrofit" existing plants on your hillside.

Individual Basins

Build up the soil on the downhill side of the plant so that any water running down the slope will pool inside the basin and soak in.

Terraces

Install header boards across the slope near the edge of the root zone and add soil to within a couple of inches of the top of the board. Be careful not to change the soil level substantially over the root zone or to pile soil against the stem.

INDEX

Page numbers in **boldface** refer to photographs.